—ᴍ—

The study of typology is much more important than the attention it has received. This is the case on several levels. First, reading Scripture rightly depends upon paying close attention to how the apostles read Scripture, which inevitably involves consideration of typology. Second, typology is a great aid in perceiving the coherence and unity of the Bible. Third, typology illuminates the uniqueness of Scripture by placing in right relation the sovereignty of God, the inspiration of Scripture and the work of God in history. Fourth, an understanding of typology enhances one's grasp of biblical theology and thus of Christian worship.

This work by Paul Hoskins is a careful and much needed guide to typology. He rightly defines it and perceptively illustrates it. Along the way, he offers assistance in reading the Fathers, knowing the difference between typology and allegory, avoiding the excesses of typology, and provides profoundly important insight into the meaning of significant biblical texts. A careful reading of this work will likely change your reading of Scripture, and without doubt for the better.

B. Paul Wolfe, PhD
Headmaster, The Cambridge School of Dallas
Formerly, Associate Professor of New Testament
Southwestern Baptist Theological Seminary

Hoskins has given us a book that is easy to read and at the same time provides fascinating insights into the treasures of the Bible. With a keen eye and able help from the Church Fathers, he traces the subtle threads of Old Testament types as they are woven into the rich tapestry of the New Testament Scriptures. This book is reliable guide into a neglected area of biblical studies.

Sigurd Grindheim, PhD
Visiting Lecturer in New Testament
Ethiopian Graduate School of Theology

We are in the midst of a healthy resurgence of interest in typology and typological interpretation, and Paul Hoskins is a reliable guide through the maze of intriguing questions and exciting possibilities. This is a book that will send you back to the Bible ready to read it again with a new curiosity about what it says and means. If you want to understand how Jesus and the Apostles read the Old Testament, you want to read this book.

James M. Hamilton Jr., PhD
Associate Professor of Biblical Theology
Southern Baptist Theological Seminary

This is a solid, substantial study of an extremely important but severely neglected theme. Hoskins presents his arguments clearly and cautiously. This is a significant work that handles the biblical evidence fairly and carefully.

Stephen Dempster, PhD
Stuart E. Murray Professor of Religious Studies
Atlantic Baptist University

In striving to understand the individual parts of Scripture, I often overlook the whole. Paul Hoskins helped me to remember that God has not only written a unified Bible, He has written a unified history. This study of typology helps us see the overarching pictures that God painted in history and in His Word. With Hoskins' clear and thorough explanations of types, our step to application of these vivid pictures will be much easier and more importantly, more accurate.

Dr. Calvin Pearson
Associate Professor of Preaching
Southwestern Baptist Theological Seminary

That Scripture Might Be Fulfilled: Typology and the Death of Christ

Paul M. Hoskins

This book is dedicated to my parents, Johnny and Ramonia.
They have been reading and correcting my
writing from the very beginning.
Thank you, Dad and Mom.

Contents

—ɯ—

Preface

—∾—

Initially began work on this book with the intention of providing an accessible introduction to typology. For those of you who are not familiar with typology, you will learn about it in chapter one. Since I have found typology to be very useful for understanding many mysterious uses of the Old Testament in the New Testament, I wanted to help others to see the benefits of typology. As I got into the project, I began to realize that my introduction to typology needed something further to unify it and keep it from growing out of control. Much of my recent writing on typology has involved the relationship between the death of Christ and the fulfillment of the Passover in the Gospel of John. This writing has influenced my seminary teaching. It has also influenced my teaching at home. Over the past few years, our family has added a new element to our celebrations at Easter time. We began to celebrate the Passover during Holy Weck. One day, it came to me. My introduction to typology should really be a book about Old Testament types of the death of Jesus. At last, I had found my focus. It is my hope that reading this book will enrich you like the preparation for it has enriched me. Perhaps you, too, will find that the subject matter increases your understanding, informs your teaching, and adds something to your worship.

This work would not have come into existence without the generous contributions of many people. First and foremost, my wife, Cheryl, has encouraged this project and aided its completion in countless ways. She has provided a number of suggestions regarding content and presentation. My children, Hannah, Timothy, and Elizabeth, also had to bear with me as I worked on this project, especially as I was trying to finish it up. I am thankful for Hannah's faithful prayers for my book. I want to give special appreciation to Dr. Sigurd Grindheim and Dr. Joshua Williams. These two colleagues read significant parts of the manuscript. They offered suggestions and encouragement. I also benefited from the suggestions of two very devoted readers, Paul Moldenhauer and Keith Woods. Finally, I want to thank those students who encouraged me to write this book, who asked good questions about typology or who shared their insights with me. God has blessed me with opportunity and insight to write this book. I pray that he will use this book to bring insight to all who read it.

Paul M. Hoskins

Chapter 1

Setting the Course

—⁂—

As I was growing up in church, I would listen to sermons and notice verses in the New Testament that contained a quotation from the Old Testament. Sometimes, in a moment of curiosity, I would flip to the Old Testament text. These efforts were usually more confusing than enlightening. The wording of the Old Testament text might be different. Worse yet, the Old Testament passage seemed to be about something unrelated. Later, I studied literature in college and began to see the New Testament's allusions to the Old Testament. At some point, I began noticing how many Psalms are quoted or alluded to in the New Testament. In some cases, Jesus was fulfilling verses from the Psalms. I thought of the book of Psalms as prayer, praise, or poetry, but not as prophecy. These were just some of the Old Testament quotations or allusions that I could not quite explain. I went to seminary and found that my confusion about the New Testament's use of the Old Testament increased. Professors and commentaries pointed to various explanations for the quotations and allusions that puzzled me. I began to think that the New Testament's use of the Old Testament was a complex issue indeed. Perhaps there was not a satisfactory way to understand it.

I was fortunate enough to go on to do doctoral work in New Testament. In my first semester, I was in a seminar taught by D. A. Carson focusing on the use of the Old Testament in the New Testament. I found myself being exposed to a line of thinking that had never surfaced clearly in my previous theological studies. As he moved from book to book in the New Testament, he was repeatedly disclosing my lack of understanding of the subject matter and my lack of preparation for grappling with a key new category, typology. I began to read everything I could find about typology and its importance for Christian interpreters through the ages. As the class ended, I could not let go of my fascination with the possibilities of typology for clarifying so many of the New Testament's mysterious quotations from and allusions to the Old Testament.

I investigated further the promise and pitfalls of typology in my dissertation on Jesus' fulfillment of the Temple in the Gospel of John. As I studied the Gospel of John and what interpreters were saying about Jesus' fulfillment of the Temple in John, I began to think that the relationship between Jesus and the Temple had the marks of a typological relationship. Yet interpreters were not inclined to use terms like "type" or "typology" for this relationship. Rather, they preferred to talk in terms of replacement or fulfillment or both. Through months of reading and study, I began to understand the baggage associated with typology. Types and typology are widely associated with fanciful interpretations of the Old Testament. For this and other reasons, traditional typology is often neglected, even by many traditional interpreters. Even so, I could not escape my sense that a traditional understanding of typology is the most appropriate way to conceptualize and explain how Jesus, a person, could fulfill a holy place, the Jerusalem Temple.

Now, I am hoping to help you on your own journey of understanding. I want you to see the possibilities that typology may hold for your understanding of the New Testament's use of the Old Testament. For instance, John 19:36 quotes Exodus 12:46 or Numbers 9:12, when it says, "Not one of his bones will be broken." This is an Old Testament law concerning the Passover lamb. How can the death of Jesus, a person, fulfill an Old Testament law concerning the Passover lamb? Or, what about the quotations from and allusions to Psalms of David that one finds in the Gospel accounts of the death of Jesus? How does Jesus fulfill verses from these Old Testament poems, especially when he is dying on the cross? For example, David appears to be talking about some experience of his own in Psalm 22:18. How could he be predicting that soldiers would cast lots for the clothes of Jesus on the cross (John 19:24-25)?

Typology is not the only way that interpreters have explained the fulfillments noted above, but it is one recognized way to account for them. It also has the merit of being an explanation that Christian interpreters have appealed to for centuries. More importantly, Christian interpreters have often claimed Jesus and the New Testament as providing the essential basis for their understanding of typology. A primary purpose of this book is to introduce you to an understanding of typology that would help you to make sense of Old Testament quotations like the ones given above.

Along the way, you will also see how attention to the fulfillment of Old Testament types enriches your understanding of New Testament teaching about the death of Jesus. Old Testament allusions and quotations work together to paint a picture of Jesus that corresponds to and fulfills the Old Testament types that point to him. Jesus stresses that he must fulfill all that the Old Testament says about him (Luke 24:44). As we look at the words of Jesus in the Gospels, we will see examples where Jesus relates his death to the fulfillment of Old Testament types. In the writings of the New Testament, we have good evidence that the apostles' interpretation of the Old Testament is rooted in the teaching of Jesus. The writings of the New Testament provide inspired portraits that show how much the apostles came to understand regarding what the Old Testament says about the death of Jesus. We often appreciate only a small portion of the apostles' findings. As a result, we miss out on some great opportunities to understand aspects of the death of Jesus for ourselves and teach these to others.

What Is Typology?

It is now time to define and describe typology. This is an important endeavor, because typology is understood and defined in a few different ways in contemporary writings. Since understanding the New Testament is our primary goal, it will be our guide as to the essential elements to include in a helpful definition and description.

Typology is the aspect of biblical interpretation that treats the significance of Old Testament types for prefiguring corresponding New Testament antitypes or fulfillments. Events (like the Exodus), persons (like David), or institutions (like the Temple) are common categories for Old Testament types. This definition brings together three related characteristics of the relationship between a type and its antitype. First, an Old Testament type prefigures its New Testament antitype. Second, in order to prefigure its antitype, a type possesses certain significant correspondences or similarities to its antitype. Third, as the fulfillment or goal of the imperfect type, the antitype will be greater than the type that anticipated it.

To clarify the points of this definition, we will start with an overview, because typology rests upon a basic understanding of God's work in history and of the inspiration of the Scriptures. In Old Testament times, God was at work shepherding and delivering his people. He was simultaneously tracing in that very work patterns or types that prefigure his later saving work in Christ, the church, the end events, and the New Jerusalem. God was also inspiring the Scriptures to be written in a way that would preserve a record of Old Testament types and anticipate their predictive significance. Furthermore, God directs the attention of his people to the future through his promises and descriptions of what their future will look like. Through his prophets, he sometimes identifies prominent people or events, like Moses, the Exodus, and David, as types (or patterns) for what he is going to do for his people in the future. Then, as Jesus brings about the climactic fulfillment of God's promises in his life, death, resurrection, and exaltation, he teaches his disciples to see how he is the fulfillment of the many promises and types that anticipated him. Jesus also teaches about the fulfillment of Old Testament promises and types in the church and their ultimate fulfillment in the end events and the New Jerusalem. The inspired accounts of what Jesus taught and what his disciples learned from him are what we have in the writings of the New Testament. Therefore, Old Testament types are an important aspect of God's progressive revelation of his plan for his people. By revealing his plan in history and Scripture, God displays his unique power to rule over and foretell the course of history.[1] Only God has this sort of control over history and insight into the future (Isaiah 46:9-11).

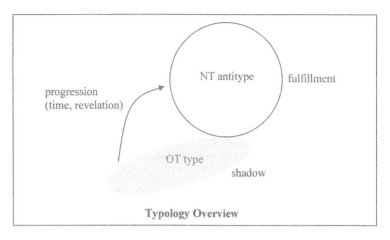

Typology Overview

In the background of the above overview lies the big picture regarding God's progressive work in history. The big picture has three important aspects. First, God is directing history along a route to an ultimate end or goal, which John portrays in his description of the end events and the New Jerusalem (Revelation 19-22). Second, the climactic step toward the ultimate goal is the work of Jesus, including his life, death, resurrection, and exaltation. Third, certain Old Testament persons, events, and institutions are important prior steps along the route to the goal. God also uses them to prefigure or foreshadow aspects of the steps that come later, especially the work of Jesus.

When it comes to understanding typology, this big picture is essential. It means that through the Old Testament types, God was accomplishing important aspects of his work. He was simultaneously using types as one of his means to predict later aspects of his work. Many types point to Christ, because he is such an important step in the big picture. One also finds types that point to the church, the end events, and the New Jerusalem, because these also lie on and conclude the route to the final realization of God's plan for his people. Jesus, the church, and the New Jerusalem are closely related.

Due to the sacrificial death of Jesus, the church is currently experiencing a good measure of the new creation life that it will experience in full in the New Jerusalem.

Another vital implication of the big picture for typology is that typology is bound up with progression toward a final goal.[2] Why is this significant? Some contemporary works define typology primarily in terms of the repetition of analogous or similar acts of God in history. Traditionally, however, interpreters have noted that the relationship between types and antitypes necessarily involves points of similarity as well as points of dissimilarity. Due to the very nature of a type (or pattern), there must be significant points of correspondence or similarity between a type and its antitype. In other words, the antitype must show noteworthy conformity to the type. Yet an antitype is not merely an analogous recurrence or repetition of the type that preceded it. The New Testament does not present the relationship between type and antitype in this way. Instead, the antitype fulfills or completes the type (Luke 22:16; John 19:24, 28) or the type is the imperfect shadow of the reality, its antitype (Hebrews 10:1).[3] Consequently, significant dissimilarities exist between type and antitype, because an antitype is going to be greater than the imperfect type that prefigured it. The antitype is the goal, fulfillment, or reality that the type anticipated.

How Does the New Testament Help Us to Understand Typology?

The authors of the New Testament provide the inspired examples of typology, which go back to the teaching of the apostles and their teacher, Jesus himself. Therefore, the most important guide for discerning genuine types and for tracing out typological relationships is the New Testament. As seen in the case of the Old Testament quotations and allusions cited in the introduction to this chapter, the New Testament

23

usually does not indicate that typology is necessary to understand the relevance of a particular Old Testament quotation or allusion. The problem is that the New Testament provides many examples of typology at work, but it does not provide a list of guidelines as to how typology works. Historically, interpreters have often attempted to provide guidelines for typology. The best guidelines are those that are truest to the New Testament examples. The New Testament examples of typology are the basis for the definition and description in the previous section, but these may require revision or clarification to represent elements of the New Testament examples better.

If the New Testament provides the authoritative examples, then careful attention to these examples is the best place to learn about typology. Instances of typology generally become apparent to the reader of the New Testament as a result of looking back at the Old Testament context of quotations from or allusions to the Old Testament. When you look at the Old Testament context, you will find there a story, statement, or description that has to do with an event, person, or institution in the history of God's people. In other words, the Old Testament passage will normally appear to have more to do with Israel's history than with prophecy regarding the future of God's people. In fact, you may find that one of the best motivations for learning about typology comes from looking at the context of Old Testament quotations found in the New Testament. You will quickly find that prophecy and fulfillment are not as straightforward as they appear to the casual reader. The following chapters will give you some practice looking at the Old Testament context of quotations and allusions.

Besides looking back at the Old Testament context of quotations, another way to get into the study of types in the New Testament is to start reading in the book of Hebrews. In Hebrews 7-10, the author presents Jesus as the antitype or fulfillment of the Old Testament priesthood and sacrifices for sin. We will look at aspects of Hebrews 9-10 in chapters five and six.

It is common for works on typology to ask whether an interpreter can find instances of typology or typological relationships that are not in some way explicitly indicated by the New Testament. The difficulty with this question is that it requires one to indicate when and how the New Testament explicitly identifies something as a type or antitype. As we have already seen, the New Testament does not generally announce to the reader that typology is necessary to understand a given Old Testament quotation or allusion. The New Testament does not appear to hold to such a guideline, especially in the case of allusions. There is probably a better way to curb the excesses that have damaged the reputation of typological interpretation.

So, what kind of controls should guide us as we look for and study typological relationships? As I mentioned above, the basic control for detecting typological relationships is to apply oneself to careful study of the New Testament's use of the Old Testament.[4] All practitioners of typology are drawing correspondences between Old Testament types and New Testament antitypes. Their source of information about each type and antitype is the Old and New Testaments. If there is a significant relationship between a certain type and antitype, then careful interpretation of relevant New Testament and Old Testament texts should produce convincing evidence for a correspondence. Convincing evidence primarily arises from examining quotations from or allusions to the Old Testament in the New Testament.[5] Of course, convincing evidence is a subjective criterion, because every interpreter gets carried away from time to time. We need a second control to provide a check on our typological interpretations. Our careful study of the New Testament's use of the Old Testament should include consulting the writings of other interpreters to see who has made the same or similar observations. Significant typological relationships should be evident to others as well.

Controls for Detecting and Studying Typological Relationships
1. Study the New Testament's use of the Old Testament.
    a. Interpret relevant texts (Old Testament and NewTestament).
    b. Examine New Testament quotes and allusions to the Old Testament.
2. Consult the writings of other interpreters.
3. When presenting results, do not state the relationship more strongly than you find it in Scripture.

A third control is probably necessary to guide us as we present the results of our study of typological relationships. We should use the New Testament as our guide to judge the strength and significance of each typological relationship. Just like allusions to the Old Testament, typological correspondences are not all equally strong, clear, and defensible. One should place more weight on allusions to the Old Testament that have more evidence in their favor. Likewise, one should also place more weight on typological relationships with good evidence to support them. It is important to note what specific points of correspondence the New Testament appears to draw between a certain type and its antitype. Just because the New Testament draws correspondences between a type and antitype in one or two areas, this does not mean that one needs to stretch to find a whole series of detailed correspondences between them. For example, a number of Church Fathers were fascinated with Joseph typology.[6] Some of them assumed a detailed typological relationship between the story of Joseph in Genesis and the life of Jesus, rather than starting with the New Testament hints of a more restrained Joseph typology. A better place to start would be with Joseph, the father of Jesus (Matthew 1-2), or Stephen's words about Joseph in Acts 7:9-16, 51. A more modest picture of the possibilities for Joseph typology emerges from these texts.

New Testament Terms Used in Typology

In addition to providing examples of typology, the New Testament is the most important source for the basic vocabulary of typology. Although the term "typology" is thought to be a relatively recent term coined by interpreters, "type" and "antitype" are both based on Greek terms that one finds in the New Testament. Several other terms are also important for the typology of the New Testament. A few notes about each term and the relevant passages in which they appear will orient the reader to this vocabulary and its usage.

"Type" is derived from the Greek term *typos*.[7] The Greek term is found 15 times in the New Testament. In three of those cases, interpreters regard its use as significant for typology. This is especially true in Romans 5:14, where Paul describes Adam as a "type of the one who was coming," namely, Jesus (5:15). Paul sets up a typological relationship between Christians and the people of Israel in 1 Corinthians 10:1-5.[8] In this context, some interpreters think that *typoi* in 10:6 and the related adverb *typikōs* in 10:11 are being used in terms of typological patterns.[9] Part of the pattern in this case is that the Israelites sinned and God judged their disobedience. The use of *typos* in Hebrews 8:5 belongs with the treatment of the next term.

"Antitype" comes from *antitypon*. *Antitypon* has to do with correspondence to a type (*typos*) and is used in 1 Peter 3:21 and Hebrews 9:24. According to one interpretation of 1 Peter 3:21, baptism is presented as the "antitype" that corresponds to the type, namely, the salvation of the eight who were delivered from death by passing through the water in Noah's ark.[10] This is the use of *antitypon* that fits with the common usage of "antitype" in writings on typology.

In Hebrews 9:24, it is used differently in that *antitypa* refers to the Tabernacle constructed by Moses. Previously, we are told that God showed Moses the "type" or "pattern" (*typos*) for the Tabernacle (Hebrews 8:5). In 9:24, the word *antitypa* is therefore used, because it indicates that the Tabernacle corresponded to the pattern or type. Thus, the Tabernacle on earth was the "antitype" to the "type" that Moses saw. This is a bit hard to explain clearly without going into more detail. Chapter five will examine Hebrews 8-9 in more detail. The basic point is that *antitypon* is consistently associated with correspondence to a *typos*, but it is not a technical term in the New Testament that conforms to its use in writings about typology.

The next two terms are also relevant to typology, because they are used several times to differentiate types from antitypes. The first term is "shadow" (*skia*). With reference to typology, it is well-known for its use in Hebrews 10:1 and Colossians 2:17. The first part of Hebrews 10:1 says that the Old Testament Law contains only the "shadow of the good things to come" rather than the things themselves. The passage goes on to show how imperfect the Old Testament sacrifices are in comparison to the sacrifice of Christ. The term "shadow" is useful for pointing to the imperfection of types in comparison to the antitypes that cast the shadow. The fact that the shadow anticipates "good things to come" suggests the predictive or prefiguring function of the Law and the types contained in it. Similarly, in Colossians 2:16-17, some of the regulations alluded to in 2:16 come from the Old Testament Law. In 2:17, Paul calls these regulations a "shadow of the things to come," whereas the "substance" belongs to Christ. The implications of the use of shadow here are analogous to its use in Hebrews 10:1.[11]

The second term commonly used to differentiate types from antitypes is "true." "True" (*alēthinos*) is sometimes used in the Gospel of John and in Hebrews to differentiate the true or complete realities from their imperfect, anticipatory shadows in the Old Testament.[12] Thus "true" sometimes distinguishes the New Testament antitypes from their Old Testament types.[13] This is probably applicable in the case of the true light (John 1:9), the true worshipers (4:23), the true bread from heaven (6:32), and the true vine (15:1).[14] It is important to note that Jesus does not devalue the importance of the Old Testament precursors for achieving God's purposes in their own time. Rather, he is claiming to bring the fullness or fulfillment that was not present in the types. A good example of this is the true bread from heaven in contrast to the manna that sustained Israel in the wilderness. Although the manna provided sustenance for the people of God when they needed food, Jesus points out that they still died (6:49). In contrast, he is the true bread from heaven that is greater than the manna, because those who eat him will not die (6:50). Similarly, in Hebrews 8:2 and 9:24, the "true tabernacle" or "true holy place" is the place where Christ enters to sprinkle his own blood in the presence of God rather than in an imperfect tabernacle on earth.

The use of "true" (*alēthinos*) to describe antitypes is consistent with the use of this adjective in English and in Greek to denote that which is real or genuine. In this case, the antitype is the real entity that fulfills the incomplete shadow that preceded it. The use of "true" (*alēthinos*) in the Gospel of John and in Hebrews probably accounts for the fact that the Greek noun *alētheia* ("truth") becomes another word for the New Testament antitypes in the works of so many Church Fathers. In these cases, *alētheia* is usually translated into English as "reality" rather than as "truth." Thus, we arrive at the common designation of the movement from type to antitype as the movement from the shadow to the reality. One commonly finds this designation in both ancient and modern discussions of typology.[15]

Of course, this is not an exhaustive account of the terms associated with typology in the New Testament. For instance, one could also consider the use of *parabolē* in Hebrews 9:9 and 11:19, where it is sometimes interpreted in terms of a model or type.[16] However, enough has been done here to introduce several important terms that have been significant for typology.

Typology, Allegory, and the Church Fathers

There has recently been a resurgence of interest in the Church Fathers, especially in relationship to biblical interpretation. At the same time, the Church Fathers are often cited as examples of poor or extravagant uses of typology and for a failure to distinguish typology from allegory. So, what value do the Church Fathers have for the student of typology? The Church Fathers provide at least two valuable areas of instruction with respect to typology. First, they provide some foils or bad examples that encourage a controlled use of typology. Second, they are the first interpreters who clarify and defend the uses of typology that one finds in the New Testament.

Regarding the Church Fathers as foils, they are the reason why so many treatments of typology are so concerned with distinguishing typology from allegory. In order to understand the weight of this concern, one needs to understand a little bit about the negative associations of allegory and about why these associations affect the legitimacy of typology. The Bible contains some allegories that are supposed to be interpreted allegorically. A good example is Jesus' parable of the sower and his interpretation of it (Matthew 13:3-9, 18-23). Jesus' interpretation shows that he regards the parable as an allegory. An allegory is basically a story whose elements represent something else. In order to interpret an allegory, one has to figure out what the elements in the story represent (see Matthew 13:18-23). In Matthew 13, Jesus provides an allegorical interpretation for three of his parables, but leaves the reader to finish the interpretation for the other parables in the chapter. This is perfectly acceptable when one is dealing with stories that are indeed allegories.

One finds a number of instances where Church Fathers interpret Old Testament historical narratives as if they were allegories with a deeper religious truth hidden in the background. In doing so, they are trying to show how certain Old Testament passages are pointing to deeper spiritual truths that go beyond the literal meaning of the passage. The problem, of course, is that the Old Testament historical narratives are not allegories and are not meant to be interpreted allegorically. Church Fathers find precedent for their allegorical approach in Philo of Alexandria, a Jew who lived in the first century. Philo is famous for providing many examples of an allegorical approach to the Old Testament. His approach is analogous to the allegorical approach used by other scholars of his time in their interpretation of other narratives, like Homer's works. These scholars felt that allegorical interpretation was especially legitimate when one was dealing with offensive or difficult passages in religious works. Church Fathers also claim the apostle Paul as a precedent due to his claim to be doing something allegorical in Galatians 4:24. However, Paul's limited use of allegory is quite different from examples of allegorical interpretation in Philo. A closer look at Galatians 4:21-31 reveals that Paul's reasoning there is primarily typological rather than allegorical. His use of the Old Testament story of Sarah and Hagar has more to do with tracing correspondences between historical persons and events than with allegorical interpretations like Philo's.[17]

Unfortunately, allegory and typology become confused with one another due to the writings of certain Church Fathers. The confusion is mostly unfortunate for typology, because the allegorical approach described above has rightly come to be regarded as suspect. Typology has therefore suffered from being lumped together with allegory. One reason for the confusion is an unfortunate choice of terminology on the part of Church Fathers who said something about how to interpret the Bible. They divided the two basic senses of Scripture into the literal sense and the spiritual sense. The spiritual sense of Scripture commonly came to be divided into three areas, one of which was the allegorical. The interpretation of types was often seen as one aspect of the allegorical sense.[18]

A second reason for the confusion is that one finds so many examples of farfetched uses of typology in the Church Fathers. These uncontrolled uses of typology look so much like their similarly creative allegorical interpretations that they become difficult to sort out.[19] One example would be the tendency to see anything cross-shaped in the Old Testament as a type of the cross, including the raised arms of Moses at the battle with Amalek (Exod 17:8-13).[20] Jean Daniélou probably provides the most helpful guide to the difference between allegorical interpretation and typological interpretation in the Church Fathers. He provides examples of both kinds of interpretation and helps one to see the fundamental differences between allegorical and typological interpretation.[21] In light of his examples of allegorical interpretation, one can see how overly creative instances of typological interpretation tend to look allegorical. However, poor typology is poor typology, it is not allegory.[22]

Now what we learn from the Church Fathers as foils or bad examples is to realize the value of establishing controls for typological interpretation. After looking at fanciful examples of typology in works by Church Fathers, one learns to value the instances of typology in the New Testament. With some exceptions, the New Testament instances of typology are readily distinguishable from allegorical interpretations and based upon significant correspondences between types and antitypes. Careful study of the types in the New Testament is the best basis for understanding typology. In fact, there are enough clear and defensible instances of typology in the New Testament to satisfy most anyone's interest in the study of types.

The Church Fathers are not just foils indicating what not to do. They can be quite helpful to us when we turn our attention to typology in the New Testament. Due to their interest in typology, one can sometimes find more attention to certain typological relationships in the Church Fathers than in recent interpreters. For instance, I was recently studying the Passover typology of the Gospel of John. I found it to be quite helpful to read the comments of Church Fathers related to the various passages where I was detecting Passover typology.[23] They sometimes showed a keener eye for connections to the Passover than more recent commentators. Their Passover homilies were also helpful. They provided pointers to Passover typology in the New Testament outside of John and examples as to how Christians have traditionally taught about the Passover and its fulfillment. I will refer to some of this material in chapter four, which focuses on the fulfillment of the Passover. I would suggest that the Church Fathers can be a valuable resource, especially when we are studying a particular typological relationship and would like to find others who have done so before us.

The Church Fathers also provide examples as to how others before us have tried to clarify the nature of typology and its usefulness for understanding the New Testament. For instance, in the second century, one finds a number of comments by Melito of Sardis on typology in his well-known homily on the Passover. Melito focuses much of his attention on the replacement of types by their antitypes, which he presents as an implication of the fact that types are by nature preparatory and incomplete (see, for instance, lines 213-79). What he says is not that much different from the book of Hebrews, but it is stated a little more sharply, perhaps due to tensions between Christians and Jews at that time. He also makes an insightful comment about the significance of types for predicting their antitypes that is worth quoting. Melito of Sardis says,

> But first the Lord made prior arrangements for his own sufferings in patriarchs and in prophets and in the whole people, setting his seal to them through both law and prophets. For the thing which is to be new and great in its realization is arranged for well in advance, so that when it comes about it may be believed in, having been foreseen well in advance. Just so also the mystery of the Lord, having been prefigured (*protypōthen*)[24] well in advance and having been seen through a model (*typon*), is today believed in now that it is fulfilled, though considered new by men.[25]

Notice that the Lord used the type or "model" to prefigure its antitype "well in advance." Since he was writing only about 150 years after Christ, the fulfillments of the types were still relatively "new." He goes on to list a number of types right after this. He concludes his list with a reference to the Passover lamb "which is slain in the land of Egypt, which struck Egypt and saved Israel by its blood" (lines 422-4). This is not surprising, since his homily is a Passover homily focused on Passover typology.[26]

In the late fourth century, John Chrysostom makes several helpful observations about typology. For example, while teaching on 1 Corinthians 10:1, he clarifies his understanding of the relationship between types and antitypes. In this case, the type is the Exodus from slavery in Egypt under Pharaoh. The antitype or reality is the Christian exodus from slavery to sin under the devil.[27] John Chrysostom says,

> Once they were delivered by the sea from Egypt; now it is from idolatry; once Pharaoh was drowned, now it is the devil; once it was the Egyptians who were suffocated, now the ancient enemy is stifled beneath our sins. You see now the relationship of the type with the [reality], and of the superiority of the latter over the former. [For, neither is it necessary for the type to be different from the reality in every respect], then there would be nothing typical. Nor has one to be identical with the other, or it would be the reality itself. . . . They were of old called to freedom; so are we: yet not to the same freedom, for ours is one far higher. Yet it is no matter for surprise that the freedom to which we are called is higher than theirs. For surely it is of the nature of the reality to excel its types, though without any opposition or contention.[28]

According to Chrysostom, then, types are going to resemble the realities or antitypes, but the realities are going to be greater than the types. He also provides an example of the use of the common typological terminology of "type" (*typos*) versus "reality" (*alētheia*).

Further examples of the helpfulness of the Church Fathers will be evident in the chapters to come, especially chapter four. As seen above, their contributions to typology serve as both an encouragement and a warning to those of us who follow in their steps.

Where Do We Go from Here?

Up to this point, we have been dealing with generalities about typology. The next step is to look at some specific instances of typology in the New Testament. The following chapters introduce the typology of the New Testament by looking at a variety of examples. In the next chapter, we will look at the role of David typology in predicting aspects of the suffering of Jesus. We will turn to the many quotations from and allusions to the Psalms, especially Psalms 22 and 69, in the Gospels' accounts of the death of Jesus. Typology having to do with the Old Testament sacrifices is widely recognized. In chapters three to six, we will see instances where Jesus' death fulfills various Old Testament sacrifices. Chapter three will focus attention on the role of typology in clarifying the words of Jesus about his body and blood at the Last Supper. In chapter four, we will trace Passover typology through the Gospel of John. Chapters five and six will look at the typology of sacrifice in Hebrews 9-10. Hebrews 9-10 is one of the highlights of sacrificial typology in the New Testament. In this way, chapters two through six will aid us in our understanding of the cross and inform our celebrations of the Lord's Supper, Passover, and Easter. This plan will help us to understand the Bible better. It will also help us to worship the Lord more fully in the Lord's Supper and at Easter, as we see how the New Testament writers use typology to point to God's plan being worked out in the death of Jesus and the redemption of his people.

Chapter 2

The Suffering of David Predicts the Suffering of Jesus the Christ

—ɯ—

W hen asked to consider the similarities between David and Jesus, students of the Bible are likely to think in terms of similarities having to do with power and authority, the kind of things that one associates with kingship. David is the great king who anticipates the even greater king, the Messiah or Christ. A closer look at the citations of the Psalms of David in the Gospels reveals an interesting similarity between David and Jesus that many students of the Bible have not considered. The Gospels contain multiple quotations and allusions to Psalms of David where David was speaking about his suffering. In fact, when one looks at the famous seven last words of Jesus from the cross, one finds that three of the seven are allusions to Psalms of David.[1] One often finds sermons on the seven last words of Jesus, but rarely finds any notice of the three Psalms of David.

The quotations and allusions to Psalms of David are especially concentrated in the chapters of the Gospels that portray Jesus' death on the cross. What accounts for this concentration? In this chapter, I will suggest that this concentration is rooted in David typology. It is already evident in the Old Testament that David is a type for the great king, the Messiah, who is to come.[2] Since David himself is a type for Jesus the Christ, David's experiences of suffering and his writing about his suffering in the Psalms provide types for the suffering of his antitype, the Christ. Of course, the sufferings of Christ at the hands of his tormentors are greater than those of David, because they lead to his death. This is what we would expect based upon the understanding of typology outlined in chapter one. The Gospel of John is the place to start for examining David typology in relationship to the suffering of Jesus, because John provides two unique instances of such typology in the teaching of Jesus during his ministry.

David's Sufferings and the Death of Jesus in the Gospel of John

David typology surfaces early in the Gospel of John in a context of opposition to Jesus (John 2:17). This anticipates a later instance of David typology that relates to his betrayal by Judas. In speaking about his betrayal by Judas, we find an instance of David typology that comes from the words of Jesus himself (John 13:18). A second instance from the teaching of Jesus occurs when he says that those who hate him are also fulfilling words from a Psalm of David (John 15:25). These examples of David typology in the Gospel of John prepare the way for two appeals to David typology that contribute to its portrayal of Jesus' fulfillment of Scripture on the cross (John 19:24, 28). These instances of David typology in the Gospel of John all point to a significant connection with the suffering of Jesus. A brief examination of them will show that these instances involve quotations from, or allusions to, a Psalm of David that Jesus, the Christ, fulfills. These are not straightforward prophecies, because they are words of David about himself. Rather, the quotations from these Psalms are part of a significant David typology that John learned from the teaching of Jesus himself.

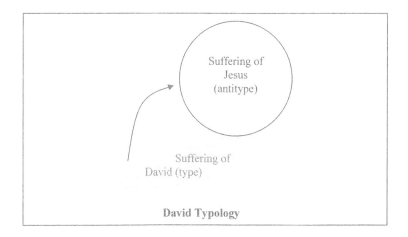

David Typology

1. "Zeal for your house will consume me." The first quotation from a Psalm of David occurs in John's account of the cleansing of the Temple. After Jesus cleanses the Temple in John 2:14-16, John 2:17 says, "His disciples remembered that it is written, 'Zeal for your house will consume me.'" If one reads this verse alongside of 2:22, the disciples probably remembered these words from Psalm 69:9 after Jesus rose from the dead.[3] They are able to understand at that point how Jesus' action in the Temple was an instance of Jesus' zeal for his Father's house. This and similar instances of Jesus' zeal for his Father's house will eventually "consume" him, which means they will lead to his death.[4] In the current context, Jesus' display of zeal for his Father's house, the Temple, provokes the "Jews" to ask for a sign (2:18). In light of similar usage elsewhere, the "Jews" refers to Jewish leaders. John apparently regards their request for a sign and their exchange with Jesus (2:18-20) as the beginning of their opposition to Jesus that will eventually consume him.[5]

As a result, John and other disciples of Jesus later come to see the exchange between Jesus and the Jewish leaders in light of the fulfillment of Psalm 69:9 (2:17). The logic of this fulfillment is best understood as typological. David, the author of Psalm 69 and the type for Jesus the Christ, wrote that his zeal for God's house consumed him.[6] In terms of similarity, Jesus' zeal for God's house consumes him as well.[7] While we do not know for sure about the gravity of David's experience, we know that his zeal for God's house did not consume him to the point of death. Jesus' experience of being consumed due to his zeal for God's house is more serious in that it leads to his death.

2. "The one who eats my bread has lifted up his heel against me." The next two quotations from Psalms of David are quite important for our purposes, because they come from Jesus himself. In John 13:18, Jesus quotes Psalm 41:9 in order to show that Judas's betrayal fulfills Scripture. Jesus says, "But it must happen so that the Scripture might be fulfilled, 'The one who eats my bread has lifted up his heel against me'" (13:18b).[8] The context beautifully illustrates Jesus' claim that one of his disciples is fulfilling this Scripture. The reader already knows that the devil has incited in Judas a commitment to betray Jesus (13:2). Shortly after 13:18, Jesus tells his disciples that one of them will betray him (13:21). Peter asks John to find out who it is. Then Jesus tells John that he will dip a morsel, probably of bread, and give it to the betrayer, which turns out to be Judas. After Judas receives the morsel, Satan enters into him and he leaves the room (13:27, 30). We see in these verses the fulfillment of Psalm 41:9 displayed right before our eyes. Jesus and Judas are sharing a meal together, as they had often done before. On this occasion, Jesus even gives a piece of bread to Judas. Judas then rises to carry out his commitment and plan to betray Jesus.

Jesus explicitly says here that Scripture is being fulfilled (John 13:18). A look at Psalm 41:9 in its context reveals that it is not a direct prophecy. In Psalm 41, David is speaking about his own experiences. He even mentions his sin in Psalm 41:4. Jesus' claim of fulfillment requires us to broaden our understanding of fulfillment to include the fulfillment of typological prophecies.[9] Some of David's words about his own experiences are prophetic, because he is the type for the great king in his line who is to come after him. As a type, then, some of his experiences prefigure or predict the experiences of his fulfillment or antitype, the Christ. David describes one of his experiences as involving a close friend who shared his bread and yet turned against him ("lifted up his heel against me") (Psalm 41:9).[10] David's words about his own experience with a friend correspond to Jesus' experience with Judas, especially in John 13. So, Jesus draws attention to the fact that the connection between the two events means that Scripture is fulfilled.[11] As was the case with John 2:17 above, Jesus' fulfillment of David's experience of suffering is more costly, because it costs him his life. David's betrayal caused him significant anguish, but apparently did not lead to his demise.

3. "They hated me without cause." Jesus once again quotes from a Psalm of David in John 15:25. He says, "But this happened so that the word that is written in their Law might be fulfilled, 'They hated me without cause.'"[12] "They hated me without cause" is a quotation from either Psalm 69:4 or 35:19. Psalm 69 is more likely due to frequent references to it through quotations or allusions in John and the other Gospels. Consequently, Jesus is using "Law" to refer to the Old Testament Scriptures as a whole, including the Psalms.[13] By doing so, he points to the fact that their Law, which is supposed to guide their behavior, predicts that some will hate the Christ without cause. Jesus is speaking about those Jews who are caught up in the sin of hating the Christ and his Father (15:24). By implication, they need to listen more carefully to their Law, in which Moses speaks about Jesus (5:46).

Many of the same things apply to this quotation from Psalm 69 as were said about the previous quotation from Psalm 41. Jesus once again uses fulfillment language with reference to a quotation from a Psalm of David. In this case, Jesus experiences the fulfillment of words of David in which David was speaking about his own experience of being hated without cause. These two examples from the teaching of Jesus help us to see why John and other disciples look for Jesus to fulfill experiences of David, especially David's experiences of opposition, betrayal, and suffering.

4. "They divided my garments" and "they cast lots." In light of John 2:17, 13:18, and 15:25, we are not surprised to see two further references to Psalms of David when Jesus is dying on the cross. Jesus' experiences of opposition and betrayal lead to his final and greatest suffering, his death on a cross. It is important to note that Pilate has already placed the title "king of the Jews" on the cross (John 19:19). In the Old Testament, the greatest king of the Jews is David. Roman soldiers are the first ones to fulfill a Psalm of David in 19:23-24. They divide Jesus' clothes among themselves, but they pause when they get to his tunic. His tunic consists of one piece of material. Rather than divide it up, they decide to cast lots for it. John then says, "These things happened so that the Scripture might be fulfilled, which says, 'They divided my garments among themselves and for my clothing they cast lots'" (19:24b).[14] John sees the soldiers' action as thoroughly fulfilling these words from Psalm 22:18. Not only do they divide his garments, but they even cast lots for one part of his clothing. Therefore, the soldiers' actions mean that Jesus again has an experience similar to an experience of David. The soldiers unwittingly help Jesus to fulfill another aspect of the type or pattern set forth in the life of David.

5. "They gave me sour wine to drink." Jesus aids the final fulfillment of a Psalm of David in John 19:28-29. John 19:28 says, "After this, when Jesus knew that all things already were accomplished, he says (so that the Scripture might be fulfilled), 'I am thirsty.'" The fulfillment of Scripture then follows in 19:29 when the soldiers give him a drink of "sour wine." This action fulfills Psalm 69:21. English translations of Psalm 69:21 generally translate the Hebrew word with "vinegar" rather than "sour wine." The Septuagint, the common Greek translation used in Jesus' time, uses the same word in Psalm 69:21 and in John 19:28, which we often translate "sour wine." So, the reader who is aware of Psalm 69:21 in the Septuagint sees another connection between the manner of the death of Jesus and David's experiences of suffering.[15]

When we look back over the ground we just covered, we see a couple of noteworthy patterns. First, Psalm 69 is given preference through two quotations (John 2:17, 15:25) and one allusion (19:28-29). One quotation comes from Psalm 41 and one from Psalm 22 (13:18, 19:24). Second, John clearly states that Jesus is fulfilling Scripture in fulfilling these verses from the Psalms. In two cases, it is Jesus himself who says that he is fulfilling Scripture (13:18, 15:25). This is important, because it is a reminder that Jesus' suffering is not merely being compared to David's suffering. A number of recent works on typology act as if typology only has to do with analogy or similarity, and separate it quite distinctly from prediction or prophecy. The fulfillment language makes it clear that Jesus is fulfilling these words concerning David's experiences. How can he fulfill words about David's experiences? The best explanation that I have encountered is that David's experiences predict the experiences of Jesus, because he provides the type or pattern for the great king who is to come after him.[16] We have already seen that the Old Testament agrees with this line of thinking.

Table 1: Summary of Quotations and Allusions to Psalms of David			
John			
1	Psalm 69:9	Zeal for your house will consume me	John 2:17 Quote
2	Psalm 41:9	The one who eats my bread has lifted up his heal against me	John 13:18 Quote, Fulfillment language
3	Psalm 69:4	They hated me without cause	John 15:25 Quote, Fulfillment language
4	Psalm 22:18	They divided my garments among themselves and for my clothing they cast lots	John 19:24b Quote
5	Psalm 69:21b	They gave me sour wine to drink	John 19:28,29 Allusion
Matthew, Mark and Luke			
6	Psalm 69:21a	They gave me gall for my food	Matthew 27:34, Mark 15:23
7	Psalm 22:18	They divided my garments among themselves and for my clothing they cast lots	Matthew 27:35, Mark 15:24, Luke 23:34

8	Psalm 22:7	All who see me mock me; they hurl insults, shaking their heads	Matthew 27:39, Mark 15:29, Luke 23:35
9	Psalm 22:8	He trusts in God. Let God deliver him now, if God delights in him	Matthew 27:43
10	Psalm 22:1	My God, my God, why have you forsaken me?	Matthew 27:46, Mark 15:34
11	Psalm 69:21b	They gave me sour wine to drink	Matthew 27:48, Mark 15:36
12	Psalm 69:21b	They gave me sour wine to drink	Luke 23:36
13	Psalm 31:5	Into your hands I commit my spirit	Luke 23:46

Overview of Allusions to Psalms of David in the Passion Narratives of Matthew, Mark, and Luke

In Matthew, Mark, and Luke, we find a somewhat different approach to connecting the sufferings of Jesus to the predictive sufferings of David. The passion narratives of these Gospels contain multiple allusions to Psalms of David, but they do not directly claim that Jesus fulfills these words of David from the Psalms.[17] The Gospel of Luke comes the closest when it records Jesus' claim that those things written about him in the Psalms must be fulfilled (24:44). Acts is more direct in that Peter specifically mentions David and calls him a prophet (1:16, 2:30). He quotes from words of David in the Psalms to show that Jesus and Judas do indeed fulfill them (1:16-20, 2:25-32). As a result, it is helpful to compare the Gospels of Matthew, Mark, and Luke to the Gospel of John and Acts. This comparison reveals the purpose of the allusions to Psalms of David in the passion narratives of Matthew, Mark, and Luke. For the alert reader, such allusions point to Jesus' fulfillment of the predictive sufferings of David.

In this section, the first goal is to point out these allusions, which are easy to miss. We will notice that Matthew, Mark, and Luke contain allusions that are not present in John. On the other hand, some of the allusions will correspond to the quotations that we saw in the Gospel of John. In these cases, John has made the connections with the Psalms more explicit. By using fulfillment language, he has helped us to connect the allusions in the other Gospels to Jesus' fulfillment of the predictive sufferings of David. Therefore, the second goal of the section will be to draw out the contribution of each allusion to our appreciation for Jesus' fulfillment of prophecy in his death. In particular, we will take special note of Jesus' allusions to Psalms of David in two of his seven last words from the cross that we find in Matthew, Mark, and Luke. In these two cases, Jesus' allusions to Psalms of David will help us to interpret the significance of his words.

6. "They gave me gall for my food." Matthew 27:34 is a good place to start. It contains the first commonly recognized allusion to a Psalm of David in Matthew's passion narrative. Matthew's passion narrative is quite similar to Mark's, but Matthew tends to bring out allusions to Psalms of David more clearly. Therefore, our focus will be upon Matthew 27 with some attention to the parallels in Mark and Luke. The first part of Matthew 27:34 says, "They gave him wine mixed with gall to drink." This is an allusion to Psalm 69:21, where David speaks about his enemies giving him "gall" for his food. One finds the same Greek word for "gall" (*cholē*) in the Septuagint and Matthew 27:34. As D. A. Carson notes, this Greek word is an appropriate translation for the Hebrew word in Psalm 69:21, because both can refer to "various bitter or poisonous substances."[18] This is important, because Mark 15:23 says that the soldiers gave him "wine mixed with myrrh" to drink instead of wine mixed with gall. Matthew is saying the same thing in different words. Myrrh is bitter, so a sufficient quantity of it would make the drink bitter. Matthew likely describes the wine that the soldiers gave to Jesus as "mixed with gall," because it correctly represents the nature of the drink as being bitter and connects this event with the words of David in Psalm 69:21. As Carson says, "The drink was offered to Jesus; it was so bitter he refused it, and, according to this view, the soldiers were amused."[19] As they were mistreating Jesus in this way, the soldiers were fulfilling Scripture at the same time. This experience of Jesus fulfills the first part of Psalm 69:21. He will fulfill the second part of that verse in Matthew 27:48.[20]

7. "They divided my garments." Next, after crucifying Jesus, the soldiers divided Jesus' clothes among themselves by casting lots for them (Matthew 27:35). In doing so, the soldiers are doing to Jesus something similar to what was once done to David according to Psalm 22:18. It is therefore common to see an allusion to Psalm 22:18 in Matthew 27:35. Mark 15:24 and Luke 23:34 are in agreement with Matthew here with only minor differences in wording. As we saw earlier, the key for interpreting the significance of this allusion is in John 19:23-24. John explicitly says in John 19:24 that the soldiers fulfilled Psalm 22:18 when they divided Jesus' garments and cast lots for his tunic.

8. "All who see me mock me." The soldiers were not the only ones to fulfill Scripture while Jesus was dying on the cross. Matthew, Mark, and Luke also present the mockers as fulfilling Psalm 22:7, where David says, "All who see me mock me; they hurl insults, shaking their heads" (NIV). Two allusions point to Psalm 22:7. First, Matthew and Mark record that those who were passing by were "shaking their heads" (Matthew 27:39, Mark 15:29). Shaking of the head is a physical expression of "mockery" that fits with the mocking words they were speaking.[21] Second, Matthew, Mark, and Luke use various Greek verbs to say that people were mocking Jesus. All of the mocking behavior described here fulfills Psalm 22:7. Luke brings out the connection between this mocking behavior and Psalm 22:7 more clearly. According to Luke, people were standing there "watching" or "looking at" Jesus. Luke uses the same Greek verb (*theōreō*) that one finds with reference to watching or looking at David in the Septuagint of Psalm 22:7. More importantly, Luke uses a rare Greek verb in Luke 23:35 (*ekmyktērizō*), when he says that the rulers "were sneering" at Jesus. The same verb occurs in the Septuagint translation of Psalm 22:7.[22]

9. "He trusts in God. Let God deliver him now, if God delights in him." Matthew goes on to show that the Jewish leaders also fulfilled Psalm 22:8, as they were mocking the crucified Jesus. In Matthew 27:43, he reports mocking words spoken by the Jewish leaders that one does not find in Mark or Luke. In all three Gospels, Jewish leaders mock Jesus for being the "King of Israel" or the "Christ" who could save others, but could not save himself from death on the cross (Matthew 27:42, Mark 15:31-32, Luke 23:35). According to Matthew, they also spoke these words, "He trusts in God. Let God deliver him now, if God delights in him, for he said, 'I am the Son of God'" (Matthew 27:43). Up until the last clause that begins with "for," the wording of this verse closely resembles the Septuagint of Psalm 22:8. Carson says that the Jewish leaders were making an "unconscious allusion" to Psalm 22:8.[23] Matthew's point would seem to be that these mocking words of the Jewish leaders are part of the David typology that runs through his passion narrative.

Their words are similar to words that were once spoken by those who were mocking David. Once again, one of David's experiences of suffering prefigures an aspect of the suffering of Jesus on the cross.

10. "My God, My God, why have you forsaken me?" The mocking words of Matthew 27:43 set the scene for the most famous and difficult to understand allusion to a Psalm of David in the passion narratives. The mockers first challenge Jesus to save himself (27:40, 42). Then, they point to the fact that he trusts in God and has claimed to be the Son of God. If so, then God should deliver him (27:43). Yet, they can plainly see that Jesus is dying with no one coming to his aid, even God. Darkness descends upon the land and then Jesus cries out, "'Ēli, ēli lema sabachthani,' that is, 'My God, my God, why have you forsaken me?'" (27:46, also Mark 15:34). This cry confirms the taunts of his enemies. Even Jesus appears to realize that God has forsaken him or left him. In order to understand Jesus' words, it is important not to neglect the fact that Jesus' words allude to Psalm 22:1, where David asked this same question.[24]

Psalm 22 begins with David's earnest question, "My God, my God, why have you forsaken me?" David then tells us that he has been crying out to God and God has not delivered him from his enemies (22:1b-2). He then recalls that his fathers trusted in God, cried out to him, and he delivered them (22:3-5). He then goes on to describe his situation (22:6-18) and to ask God for deliverance (22:11, 19-21). Next, he expresses confidence in God's salvation (22:22-24). Psalm 22 is similar to other cases in the Psalms. In a general sense, David recognizes that God does not forsake the righteous, and that he delivers them from the wicked (Psalm 37:28, 39-40; 9:10). Yet David still prays for God not to forsake him and to hasten to deliver him from his enemies (Psalm 38:19-22, 71:10-12). When we look at these points together, we see that David believes that God will not forsake the righteous, so David's belief gives him confidence to pray to God for deliverance when his enemies pose a threat. An important thing to notice is what we learn here about being forsaken or abandoned by God. In these Psalms, abandonment by God would mean that God does not, or has not, come to deliver his child from the enemies.[25] In Psalm 22:1-21, David is having an experience of being forsaken by God. He is enduring ongoing threats and persecutions from his enemies and he is praying for God to come and deliver him. In Psalm 22:1, the Psalmist's question is a cry of "lamentation over prolonged desertion by God," his deliverer. [26] It expresses his sense of "alienation" from God and "yearning" for God and deliverance.[27]

When Jesus speaks the same words (Psalm 22:1), he does so in the midst of an analogous and even worse predicament. His opponents have mocked him, like they mocked David (Psalm 22:6-8). His opponents have divided his clothes among themselves, like they did to David (Psalm 22:18). His very life is slipping away in the presence of his opponents, whereas David suffered at the hands of his opponents, but they did not kill him. In the midst of this, Jesus is experiencing abandonment by his Father, who is not coming to deliver him from death at the hands of his persecutors. It is no wonder that the words of Psalms 22:1 give voice to his cry to the Father at this moment. They give voice to his sense of abandonment by God and yearning for deliverance.[28] He is at his lowest point, nearing imminent death, which he must pass through rather than simply escape from it. However, Psalm 22 reminds the reader that there is hope. Just as God eventually delivers David, so also God will deliver Jesus the Christ from death through the resurrection. It is important to come back to Jesus' fulfillment of the Scriptures in this moment. Christ's very experience of abandonment by God fulfills the Scriptures in that he is having an experience that fulfills a previous experience of David. Then, Christ speaks the words that David spoke when he was having a similar experience. In doing so, he draws attention both to his abandonment by God and to his fulfillment of an experience of David.

11. "They gave me sour wine to drink." Matthew's account then adds one more allusion that brings us back to the allusion with which we started in Matthew 27:34. Some who hear Jesus' words think that he is calling for Elijah rather than for God when he says, "Ēli" (Matthew 27:46, Mark 15:35). Someone gives him "sour wine" to drink from a "sponge" (Matthew 27:48, Mark 15:36). This action fulfills Psalm 69:21. As seen above in reference to John 19:29, the same Greek word translated "sour wine" is used in the Septuagint of Psalm 69:21 and here in Matthew 27:48.[29]

12. "They gave me sour wine to drink." The final two allusions that we need to consider come from Luke. Luke 23:36 probably provides Luke's somewhat unique account of the drink that the soldiers gave to Jesus in Matthew 27:34 and Mark 15:23. In Matthew and Mark, the drink was wine mixed with gall or myrrh. Luke only refers to this one drink rather than to two drinks being given to Jesus (Matthew 27:34, 48). In combining these two, Luke apparently omits the reference to gall or myrrh. He also refers to the drink as "sour wine" rather than as just "wine" (see Matthew 27:34). In this way, Luke still brings out one allusion to Psalm 69:21, and omits the second one (Matthew 27:48). This is not surprising, since Luke does not contain Jesus' allusion to Psalm 22:1 (Matthew 27:46). He may have had his own reasons for alluding only to the "sour wine" in Psalm 69:21 and not to the gall.

13. "Into your hands I commit my spirit." For the last allusion, we return to the words of Jesus once again. In Luke 23:46, we find the last words of Jesus according to Luke. It says, "And Jesus said, crying out with a loud voice, 'Father, into your hands I commit my spirit.' And after he said this, he breathed his last" (23:46). Jesus here prays to his Father with words that allude to Psalm 31:5. In light of what we have seen before, we are not surprised to find that this is a Psalm attributed to David. Luke 23:46 is a report of Jesus' final prayer. Since Luke shows Jesus praying more often than the other Gospels do, it is fitting that Jesus' last words in Luke take the form of a prayer.[30] As we saw with Matthew 27:46 ("My God, my God, why have you forsaken me?"), looking at Psalm 31 will probably help us to interpret Jesus' last words in Luke 23:46.

Psalm 31 is similar to Psalm 22. David speaks of his trials and especially of the threat that he faces from his opponents. They are seeking to take his life (31:13). David prays for deliverance (31:1-2, 15-18). In much of the rest of the Psalm, David expresses in various ways his confidence in God as his deliverer who will answer his prayers (see especially 31:3-5). Therefore, interpreters commonly read "Into your hands I commit my spirit" in 31:5 as an expression of trust in God for saving him from death at the hands of his enemies.[31]

When Jesus speaks words from Psalm 31:5 on the cross, interpreters think that he could mean two things by them. He could simply be expressing his trust in God. Even though he is about to die at the hand of his enemies, he still trusts in God and commits his spirit into his Father's hands.[32] Other interpreters think that we can go further than this based on the context of Psalm 31:5 in Psalm 31. Jesus could be saying these words as an expression of trust in God as his deliverer, because he believes that God will yet deliver him from death through the resurrection.[33] After all, Jesus already predicted his resurrection (Luke 9:22, 18:33). Peter later quotes from another Psalm of David, Psalm 16, to show that David's words there predict the resurrection of the Christ (Acts 2:24-32, 13:35-37).[34] So, Jesus' last words in Luke surely express complete trust in God in the face of death. It is also possible that they express his faith that God will yet vindicate him and reveal himself as his deliverer through the resurrection. In other words, Jesus' last words in Luke may express his faith that his death is not the end of the story. They may anticipate the hope of the resurrection, which is prevalent in the next chapter of Luke (24:7, 26, 46).[35]

In relation to David typology, it is possible to see how Jesus has an experience that corresponds to and yet goes beyond an experience of David. Like David, Jesus committed his spirit into God's hands at a time when his persecutors were seeking his life. Yet Jesus' experience goes beyond David's in at least two respects.[36] First, Jesus speaks the words of Psalm 31:5 when death is imminent and not just anticipated or feared (Psalm 31:13). Second, because of this timing, it seems possible that Jesus' expression of faith points to his confidence that God will yet deliver him from his persecutors through the resurrection.

Now, in light of our overview, what patterns can we see in the allusions to Psalms of David? An allusion to Psalm 69:21 occurs in Matthew, Mark, and Luke. Matthew goes out of his way to allude to it twice (27:34, 48). As far as number of allusions, Psalm 22 is the clear favorite with allusions to four of its verses (22:1, 7, 8, 18). Allusions to Psalm 22:7 and 22:18 occur in all three Gospels. In Matthew and Mark, the last reported words of Jesus allude to Psalm 22:1. In Luke, Jesus' last words allude to Psalm 31:5. When we include John, we find that all four Gospels quote or allude to Psalm 22:18 and 69:21. Thus, all four include the soldiers' unwitting fulfillment of Scripture when they divided Jesus' garments and gave him sour wine to drink. Together, the Gospels point out several aspects of the death of Jesus that correspond to and fulfill words that David wrote about his experiences of suffering. This connection between the suffering of David and the suffering of Jesus is surely worthy of a little more reflection.

Reflection and Conclusion

What difference does it make for us to be able to recognize references to Psalms of David in the passion narratives of Matthew, Mark, Luke, and John? In a few cases, we have seen that studying the words of David in their contexts helps us to interpret the significance of the words of Jesus. This is especially true with respect to "My God, my God, why have you forsaken me?" and "Into your hands I commit my spirit." We have also seen that the references to Psalms of David provide evidence that Jesus was fulfilling the Scriptures, as he was dying on the cross.

It is important to dwell on the fact that his suffering fulfills aspects of the suffering of his type, David. When we do so, we realize the irony in the words written on the cross above Jesus' head and echoed in the taunts of the mockers. Recall that the sign on the cross says that Jesus is "the King of the Jews." In Matthew, Mark, and Luke, the mockers call him "the King of the Jews" or "the King of Israel" and challenge him to save himself. In Mark and Luke, the mockers also call him the "Christ," while in Matthew they call him the "Son of God." Both of these are titles for the expected great king in the line of David, the Messiah.

These are all words that are applied to Jesus in a spirit of ridicule, including the sign on the cross. Yet, the irony in these words is that they are actually truer of Jesus than of any previous king of God's people. Jesus could have come down from the cross and saved himself. His power and authority is greater than that of any King of Israel. Jesus shows that he is the true King of Israel, because he faithfully suffers like David and even more than David. For those with eyes to see, Jesus suffers and dies as the true Son of David. Like David, Jesus is obedient to God, a man after God's own heart (1 Samuel 13:14). His obedience leads to suffering and death. As we will see in the coming chapters, his humble death saves his people from sin, death, and the power of the devil. The Good Shepherd saves his people by laying down his life for his sheep (John 10:11). Here is great power clothed in humility. Christ's death overcomes the world and the devil (John 12:31, 16:33). What a Savior is Christ, our Lord.

Dwelling on Christ's fulfillment of David's pattern of suffering draws our attention to the uniqueness of God and his plan. Part of God's plan for David's life was for David to suffer and for David to write about his suffering in such a way as to anticipate specific aspects of the suffering of Jesus, the Christ. Christian interpreters have long been impressed, for instance, with the significant correspondences between aspects of Psalm 22 and the suffering of Jesus on the cross. The correspondences have so impressed a number of interpreters that they can only see Jesus in Psalm 22 and deny most all of its relevance for David's suffering.[37] The impressive correspondences are the result of God's unique power to plan and guide the course of history (Isaiah 46:9-11). God inspired David to write Psalm 22:18 centuries before he brought to pass the death of Christ on the cross in a setting where the soldiers would divide Christ's clothing among themselves. The soldiers were completely unaware that they were willingly fulfilling God's plan for the death of his Son, Jesus Christ.

Chapter 3

Jesus' Words at the Lord's Supper in Light of the Old Testament Sacrifices

—∽∾—

In church, Christians hear certain key words repeated over and over again. One of those sets of key words is the words that Jesus spoke at the Lord's Supper or Last Supper. Jesus commanded us to celebrate this supper until he comes. Therefore, we celebrate it regularly, and repeat the words that Jesus spoke on that historic night with his disciples. In many cases, we receive only basic instruction regarding the meaning of Jesus' words. We therefore miss out on the richness of Jesus' words. On closer inspection, it turns out that his words at the Last Supper are rich with allusions to Old Testament sacrifices. He is pointing to his sacrificial death as the true sacrifice that fulfills at least three sacrifices. By studying those sacrifices, we can increase our understanding of what Jesus is saying about his sacrificial death. Consequently, the Lord's Supper will have more meaning for us, which will enrich our worship and our instruction of others.

In this chapter, we will examine Jesus' words at the Last Supper closely. His words at the Last Supper are a compressed form of teaching. Jesus has woven together three related typologies into his brief words. All three typologies have to do with the Old Testament sacrifices and complement one another. Like the Old Testament sacrifices of atonement (typology one), Jesus' blood is poured out to secure the forgiveness of his people's sins. Like the covenant inauguration sacrifices of Exodus 24 (typology two), Jesus' blood sanctifies his people so that they might become part of the new covenant people of God. Like the Passover sacrifice and feast (typology three), Jesus calls upon his disciples to eat his body and drink his blood in remembrance of the salvation that he secured by his death. Thus, at the very heart of Jesus' words at the Last Supper lies the salvation and sanctification of the new covenant people of God in fulfillment of these three Old Testament sacrifices. We will begin with the sacrifices of atonement.

The Last Supper and the Old Testament Sacrifices of Atonement

Jesus' words about his blood will be the focus of this section. They are the key words in which he alludes to the Old Testament sacrifices of atonement. Matthew's account of Jesus' words is particularly significant in this regard. Matthew 26:28 contains significant connections to Leviticus 4-6. Leviticus 4-6 describes the sacrifices often known as the "sin offering" and the "guilt offering." These are not the only sacrifices associated with making atonement in Leviticus, but they are prominently associated with it. This is especially true of the sin offering due to its central place in the rituals of the Day of Atonement (Leviticus 16). We will look first at the strength of the connections between the words of Jesus at the Last Supper and the descriptions of the sacrifices in Leviticus 4-6. Then, we will factor in the importance of Isaiah 53 as a unique Old Testament pointer to Jesus' fulfillment of the atonement sacrifices. Finally, we will anticipate that Jesus' death simultaneously fulfills sacrifices of atonement outside of those in Leviticus 4-6, including the Passover sacrifice.

Before looking at the words of Jesus, it may be helpful to explain a few key terms. For our purposes, sacrifices of atonement are sacrifices that the Old Testament connects with "making atonement." "Make atonement" is a common translation for a particular Hebrew verb.[1] Perhaps the best way to explain what it means to "make atonement" is to say that it usually means "to accomplish reconciliation between God and man."[2] Why do you suppose that it is necessary to accomplish reconciliation between God and man (to make atonement)? The Old Testament provides two primary answers, namely, sin and impurity (or uncleanness). For example, we find these two answers related to the need for making atonement on the Day of Atonement (Leviticus 16:16). It is therefore not surprising to find a connection between making atonement and forgiveness of sin in Leviticus 4-6. In these chapters, the priest makes atonement for the sinner through the sin offering or the guilt offering and God forgives his sin (for example, Leviticus 4:35).

We are now ready to look at Jesus' words regarding his blood. In Matthew 26:28, Jesus says, "For this is my blood of the covenant, which is poured out for many for the forgiveness of sins." Mark 14:24 says the same thing, but does not include "for the forgiveness of sins." According to Luke 22:20, Jesus says, "This cup is the new covenant in my blood, which is poured out for you." In all three Gospels, Jesus speaks about the pouring out of his blood. In Matthew and Mark, his blood is poured out "for many," while in Luke it is poured out "for you." According to Matthew, Jesus says that his blood is poured out "for the forgiveness of sins." These words add to an impression already created by the mention of blood of the covenant and pouring out of his blood for others. Jesus is here using language about his blood that recalls the sacrifices of the Old Testament. He is presenting himself as the antitype who fulfills those sacrifices. To demonstrate this, we will look first at the pouring out of blood and forgiveness of sins in relation to the sacrifices of atonement in Leviticus.

With respect to pouring out blood, it is important to note that pouring out or shedding blood is a common way to speak about killing a person in the Old Testament (Genesis 9:6, for example). On one level, when Jesus talks about his blood being poured out for many, he is simply saying that he will be killed for many. The first hint that Jesus means something more than this is found just prior to the mention of pouring out blood in Matthew 26:28. Jesus calls his blood "blood of the covenant." This is not a common phrase in the Old Testament. It is uniquely associated with the blood of the covenant sacrifices in Exodus 24:8. So, Jesus begins his words about his blood by referring to his blood as the blood of a covenant sacrifice.

The blood of a sacrifice is special. God's people are supposed to avoid eating the blood of any animal that they kill, because all animal blood is sacred. It is sacred, because blood is used for making atonement on God's altar (Leviticus 17:10-13). Consequently, God's people are supposed to pour out the blood of every animal that they kill, and especially of every sacrifice. When an animal is sacrificed, its blood is not just poured out somewhere on the ground like other animals (Leviticus 17:13). The Law tells the priest what to do with the blood of each type of sacrifice. In the case of the sin and guilt offerings of Leviticus 4-6, the priest takes some of the blood in a basin and applies it to the altar and sometimes to other parts of the Tabernacle as well. He pours out the rest of the sacrificial animal's blood at the base of the altar. Leviticus 4 repeatedly mentions the pouring out of the blood of the sin offerings at the base of the altar (4:7, 18, 25, 30, 34; also 5:9). Thus, when it comes to sin and guilt offerings, the pouring out of the blood of the sacrificial animal is part of the sacrificial ritual. This is true for peace offerings as well, but not for burnt offerings, whose blood is burned up (Deuteronomy 12:27). In Matthew, Mark, and Luke, Jesus uses the same Greek verb for pouring out, when he speaks about the pouring out of his blood. It is the Greek verb that one finds in the Septuagint with reference to pouring out a person's blood (i.e., killing a person) and to pouring out the blood of a sacrifice.[3]

Besides the prior mention of the covenant sacrifice, we know that Jesus is not merely saying that someone will kill him due to the words that modify "poured out." The first modifier is the phrase "for many" (Matthew and Mark) or "for you" (Luke). Leviticus 4-6 periodically repeats a significant set of words as it describes what is accomplished through sacrificing the sin offering and the guilt offering. It concludes its description of each sacrifice by saying something like this: Through the sacrifice, the priest makes atonement for a person or group and that the person or group is forgiven (for example, 4:20). In a couple of places, a longer formula occurs, which says, "In this way the priest will make atonement *for him for the sin* he has committed, and he will be forgiven" (4:35b [NIV, my emphasis]; also 5:10). Note that these words follow immediately after the description of the sacrifice (Leviticus 4:32-35a). Now, when Jesus says that his blood is poured out "for many," he appears to mean that his blood is poured out in order to make atonement for many, for their sins.[4] Matthew 26:28 is closer once again to the wording of the Septuagint in Leviticus 4-6, because he has chosen the same Greek preposition (*peri*, "for") that one finds in verses like Leviticus 4:35.

The first modifier, "for many," does not necessarily have to mean that Jesus' blood would be poured out to make atonement for others. It could just indicate that Jesus saw himself as dying for the sake of others in some general way.

It is the addition of the second modifier in Matthew 26:28 that significantly strengthens the connection between Jesus' words and Leviticus 4-6.[5] Matthew's second phrase that modifies "poured out" is "for the forgiveness of sins." As seen in the previous paragraph, Leviticus 4-6 says repeatedly that the priest makes atonement and the person is forgiven. This means that the person is forgiven for the sin for which the sacrifice was offered. The Septuagint of Leviticus 4:20 makes this explicit by ending this way: "... and the sin will be forgiven to them." As it turns out, the key allusion to Leviticus 4-6 is not the pouring out of Jesus' blood or its first modifier, "for many." The key allusion in Matthew 26:28 consists in the combination of "blood," "poured out," "for" someone, and "forgiveness of sins." Nowhere else in the Old Testament does one find a passage with the combination of these elements like Leviticus 4-6. Of particular importance, Leviticus 4-6 uniquely connects making atonement and forgiveness of sins.

Upon reading Leviticus 4-6, one finds that it provides significant background for Jesus' words about his blood. These chapters provide the Old Testament's most substantial treatment of the sin offering and the guilt offering, which are probably the two most significant sacrifices of atonement in the Old Testament. Jesus, to be sure, does not mean for his blood to be merely the equivalent to these sacrifices. He means for his blood to be their decisive antitype and fulfillment.[6] How can the blood of sacrificial animals possibly compare in its significance to the blood of the Son of God?

To answer this question, it is important to appreciate how Isaiah 53 prepares the way for Jesus to be the antitype and fulfillment to the sacrifices of Leviticus 4-6. Leviticus 4-6 is rarely highlighted in commentaries and other works on Jesus' words about his blood (Matthew 26:28, Mark 14:24, and Luke 22:20). With respect to Matthew and Mark, a focus on Isaiah 53 tends to steal the show. Why is this? It is probably because Isaiah 53 is such a highly regarded Old Testament passage for Christian interpreters. To Christians, Isaiah 53 reads like a clear prophecy of the death of Christ. What is the nature of the connection between Isaiah 53 and the words of Jesus about his blood?

There is not a strong connection in terms of common language. Isaiah 53 makes only a minor unique contribution to the words of Jesus in Matthew 26:28 or Mark 14:24. Isaiah 53:11-12 twice contains the word "many" and uses it in a sense similar to what one finds in Matthew 26:28.[7] One does not find "many" anywhere in Leviticus 4-6. On the other hand, Isaiah 53 does not explicitly mention blood or forgiveness of sins. According to some English translations like the New International Version, Isaiah 53:12 speaks about pouring out the Servant's life. The Septuagint version does not contain any reference to pouring out in its translation of 53:12. In terms of language, then, Isaiah 53 appears to contribute only one of the specific words of Jesus at the Last Supper.

The connection between Isaiah 53 and the words of Jesus about his blood is actually more significant than the shared language shows. Isaiah 53 is an important passage for predicting the death of Jesus, because of its distinctive contribution to the Old Testament's typology of atonement sacrifices. Isaiah 53 is the most noteworthy place in the Old Testament where a person's death is described in terms reminiscent of a sacrifice of atonement. The Servant bears the sins of many (53:11-12) and he dies as a "guilt offering" (53:10). Isaiah 53 is rightly emphasized in the teaching of the New Testament. [8] According to Isaiah 53, God's Servant, rather than a sacrificial animal, dies for the sins of many. Isaiah 53 is a direct prophecy. It is an important Old Testament prediction that helps to connect the sacrifices of atonement to their ultimate fulfillment in the death of Jesus. In other words, Isaiah 53 is an important point along the way as one progresses from the Old Testament type to the New Testament antitype. Isaiah 53 predicts a time when God's people will benefit from the sacrificial, atoning death of God's Servant. Jesus' death fulfills Isaiah 53 and the broader typology of atonement sacrifices to which Isaiah 53 contributes.

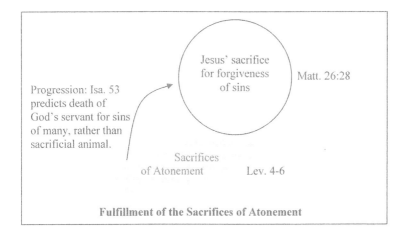

Progression: Isa. 53 predicts death of God's servant for sins of many, rather than sacrificial animal.

Jesus' sacrifice for forgiveness of sins

Matt. 26:28

Sacrifices of Atonement

Lev. 4-6

Fulfillment of the Sacrifices of Atonement

As is the case with the David typology that we look at in other chapters, various passages in the Old Testament contribute to the typology of atonement sacrifices that ultimately finds its fulfillment in the sacrificial death of Jesus. At the Last Supper, Jesus' words about his blood allude to two important contributors to this typology, namely, Leviticus 4-6 and Isaiah 53. While Leviticus 4-6 is the stronger allusion in terms of similar language, Isaiah 53 is an important contributor as well, because it provides an example where a person's death is spoken about in sacrificial terms. Through his words about his blood, Jesus presents his sacrificial death as the ultimate fulfillment of the Old Testament sacrifices of atonement and of Isaiah 53.

We need to add a word of caution here. We have seen how Jesus' words about his blood allude to Leviticus 4-6. Note that I have tried to focus more on the fulfillment of the Old Testament sacrifices of atonement rather than narrowly on fulfillment of the sin offering and guilt offering of Leviticus 4-6. This is quite intentional. Jesus' words about his blood allude to Leviticus 4-6, because they make a unique contribution to Old Testament teaching on sacrifices of atonement. They uniquely tie making atonement to forgiveness of sin. It is difficult to know how tightly to tie Jesus' words about his blood to the fulfillment of the sin offering and the guilt offering. We are going to see that Jesus' words at the Last Supper point to a couple of sacrifices. For instance, we are going to learn about the blood of the covenant and the Passover sacrifice. These sacrifices are primarily associated with sanctification, but they also make atonement and are therefore related to the forgiveness of sins. The Gospel of John primarily relates Jesus' blood to the fulfillment of the Passover sacrifice. Hebrews 9-10 relates Jesus' blood to the fulfillment of the sin offering. It is probably safe to say that Jesus' words about his blood point to his fulfillment of the Old Testament's typology of sacrifices of atonement. Leviticus 4-6 and Isaiah 53 both make unique contributions to this typology.

When we repeat Jesus' words about his blood at the Lord's Supper, we are repeating Jesus' pointers to the significance of his death for us. His death was a sacrificial death, which he had to die in order to fulfill the Old Testament sacrifices of atonement. As their ultimate fulfillment, he is our sacrifice of atonement or propitiation, whose blood makes atonement for us so that our sins can be forgiven (Romans 3:21-25, 1 John 1:5-2:2). The true significance of making atonement and forgiveness of sin is reconciliation to God. Sin alienates us from God. Jesus offers his blood to reconcile us and bring us to God (Colossians 1:21-22, 1 Peter 3:18). As we will see below, his fulfillment of the sacrifices of atonement also means that his blood cleanses us from sin and sanctifies us (1

John 1:9, Hebrews 13:12). As David says, "How blessed is he whose transgression is forgiven, Whose sin is covered!" (Psalm 32:1, NIV).

The Last Supper and the Inauguration of the Covenant in Exodus 24

Jesus' words about his blood allude to a second typology that complements the first. When Jesus speaks about his blood as the "blood of the covenant," he is alluding to Exodus 24:8. In Exodus 24:8, the "blood of the covenant" is part of ratifying the covenant between God and Israel. This blood is the blood of sacrifices (24:5-8). In Exodus and Leviticus, the blood of sacrifices is closely associated with making atonement, sanctifying, and cleansing from sin and impurity.[9] The "blood of the covenant" in Exodus 24:8 should probably be associated with all three of these as well. Among these, it is especially significant with respect to sanctification. The blood of the covenant sanctifies Israel.

As a result of their sanctification, they become God's holy people. Similarly, when Jesus speaks about his blood as blood of the covenant, he likely means that his blood sanctifies believers so that they become God's holy people under the new covenant. When he speaks about his blood in relation to the new covenant, Jesus appears to be alluding to both Exodus 24 and Jeremiah 31:31-34. Exodus 24 is the primary Old Testament text. Jeremiah 31, like Isaiah 53 above, is a direct prophecy that contributes to the Old Testament's covenant typology. Jeremiah 31 predicts a new covenant and describes a few of its unique characteristics. To clarify and support these points, we will look again at Jesus' words about his blood and their connections to the Old Testament. We will then examine how these connections help us to understand the significance of Jesus' words for the new covenant people of God.

Table 2: Summary of the Words of Jesus at the Last Supper			
Words of Jesus at Last Supper	**Old Testament Sacrifice (type)**	**Old Testament Text(s)**	**Benefit(s) of the Sacrificial Death of Christ (antitype)**
For this is my <u>blood</u> of the covenant, which is <u>poured out for</u> many <u>for the forgiveness of sins</u>. (Matt. 26:28)	Sacrifices of Atonement	Lev. 4-6	Atonement for sin
For this is my blood of the covenant, which is poured out for <u>many</u> for the forgiveness of sins. (Matt. 26:28)	Death of the Suffering Servant, who dies as a "guilt offering"	Isa. 53	Atonement for sin
For this is my <u>blood of the covenant</u>, which is poured out for many for the forgiveness of sins. (Matt. 26:28)	Blood of the Covenant	Exod. 24:8	Sanctification

This cup is the <u>new covenant</u> in my blood, which is poured out for you. (Luke 22:20)	No sacrifice explicitly mentioned in Jer. 31:31-34	Jer. 31:31	New covenant between God and his people
This is my <u>body, which is given for you;</u> do this in remembrance of me. (Luke 22:19)	Common sacrificial language	Ps. 51:16, Lev. 1:2 (see Luke 2:24)	
<u>This is my body,</u> which is given for you; do this in remembrance of me. (Luke 22:19) Take, <u>eat; this is my body.</u> (Matt. 26:26)	Passover sacrifice	Exod. 12:8	Celebrate deliverance from death and slavery through the sacrificial death of Christ
This is my body, which is given for you; <u>do this in remembrance of me.</u> (Luke 22:19)	Passover sacrifice	Exod. 12:14	Remember deliverance from death and slavery through the sacrificial death of Christ

In Matthew 26:28 and Mark 14:24, Jesus begins his words about his blood by saying, "This is my blood of the covenant." In Luke 22:20, Jesus says, "This cup is the new covenant in my blood." In both cases, Jesus speaks about a covenant that he relates to his blood. "Blood of the covenant" is a distinctive phrase that only occurs twice in the Old Testament, in Exodus 24:8 and Zechariah 9:11. Zechariah 9:11 looks like a reference back to Exodus 24:8. As we have seen previously, Matthew chooses to use language that is very close to the language of the Septuagint, which makes it easier to detect allusions to the Old Testament. Luke 22:20 adds the word "new" to covenant. The phrase "new covenant" occurs in the Old Testament only in Jeremiah 31:31. Matthew and Mark do not contain the adjective "new." "New" is probably implied, because Jesus is clearly instituting something new here. According to Luke, this new covenant is "in my blood." Instead of this translation, the Complete Jewish Bible says the new covenant is "ratified by my blood" in order to bring out the connection with Exodus 24.

If Jesus is presenting his blood as the fulfillment of the "blood of the covenant," we need to have some understanding of the original "blood of the covenant" in Exodus 24. This is more difficult than it sounds, because we find out very little about the blood of the covenant from Exodus 24. At Moses' command, young men offer burnt offerings and peace offerings (24:5). Moses takes the blood and divides it into two parts. He sprinkles half of the blood on the altar (24:6). Moses reads God's words from the "book of the covenant" and the people pledge their obedience to God's words (24:7). Then, Exodus 24:8 says, "Moses then took the blood, sprinkled it on the people and said, 'This is the blood of the covenant that the LORD has made with you in accordance with all these words'" (NIV).

One key to understanding the blood of the covenant is to look back a few chapters to the beginning of the events that lead to the covenant ratification ceremony in Exodus 24. In Exodus 19:3-6, God introduces his covenant to Israel. Among other things, he says that if they obey him and keep his covenant, then they will be his special people, "a kingdom of priests," and "a holy nation" (19:5-6). Later, in Exodus 24:7-8, the twelve tribes of Israel commit themselves to obeying God's words and Moses sprinkles them with the blood of the covenant. Presumably, the ratification of the covenant with blood marks their entry into the covenant with God. As a result, they become God's kingdom of priests and a holy nation. Now, being holy means that someone is "dedicated to the service of God."[10] In Exodus and Leviticus, to sanctify someone or something means to make someone or something holy.[11] Sanctification often takes place through the blood of sacrifices. It is therefore reasonable to suggest that the blood of the covenant sanctified Israel, that is, it made them holy.

If God's people are a kingdom of priests as well, then we are not surprised by the significant similarities between the sanctification of Israel and the special sanctification of the priests in Exodus 29 and Leviticus 8. The sanctification of the priests includes the sacrifice of a burnt offering and of a special "ordination ram," which is basically a special form of peace offering (Exodus 29:15-34).[12] Unlike a normal peace offering, some of the ordination ram's blood is applied to the priests' right ears, thumbs, and toes. Some is also sprinkled on the priests along with special anointing oil. These applications of blood sanctify the priests and their garments so that they are holy (29:21).[13] Exodus 29:33 later adds that the ram of ordination makes atonement for the priests to sanctify them. It is unusual in the Old Testament to see peace offerings associated with sanctification or making atonement. We would normally think of sin offerings as sanctifying and making atonement, like they do on the Day of Atonement (Leviticus 16, also 8:14-15). The description of the ordination ram provides an important instance where a peace offering makes atonement and sanctifies. If it does these two things, then one can probably assume that it cleanses from sin and impurity as well in light of the close relationship between these three (Leviticus 8:15, 16:18-19).[14]

Note two important similarities between the sanctification of the priests and the sanctification of Israel. Both cases involve burnt offerings and peace offerings. In both cases, Moses does something unusual. He applies some of the blood of the sacrifices to the priests or Israel. If the application of blood is clearly said to sanctify the priests, then this would seem to be good evidence that the blood of the covenant sanctified Israel.[15] Similarly, as was the case with the priests, it probably made atonement for them and cleansed them from sin and impurity at the same time.

Before we move on to speak about Jesus' fulfillment of the blood of the covenant, we should quickly review and reinforce the points that we just covered. We noticed two important aspects of the blood of the covenant in Exodus 24:8. First, it is part of the ratification of the covenant between God and Israel. The ratification of the covenant is not all that is involved however. At a later renewal of the covenant, one finds mention of peace offerings, but never again is there mention of the application of blood of the covenant to the people (Deuteronomy 27). There must be a second aspect to the significance of the blood of the covenant. Based on the evidence above, the blood of the covenant sanctifies Israel so that they become God's holy people.

When we look to the New Testament and Jesus' fulfillment of the blood of the covenant, it is the book of Hebrews that contains the most attention to this matter. Hebrews mentions the original blood of the covenant in Hebrews 9. He says that it was part of the inauguration of the first covenant (9:18). He goes on to mention the blood of the covenant as blood that sanctifies the people of God (10:29). These verses seem to suggest that the author of Hebrews understands Jesus' fulfillment of the blood of the covenant in a way that fits nicely with the understanding of the blood of the covenant described above.

Having looked at "blood of the covenant" from Exodus 24, we now need to see what the allusion to "new covenant" in Jeremiah 31:31 adds to our understanding of the words of Jesus at the Last Supper. As we saw earlier, this allusion is explicit in Jesus' words in Luke 22:20. Jeremiah 31 is a bit like Isaiah 53 in that it is a direct prophecy that reveals some important things about God's plan for his people. To begin with, it reveals that God anticipates a time when he will establish a "new" covenant with his people. Jeremiah 31:31-34 then describes the new covenant in ways that distinguish it from the old covenant, which Israel and Judah broke (31:32). In the case of the new covenant, God's law will be in his people, written on their hearts (31:33). All of God's people will know him and he will forgive their sins (31:34). This is a noteworthy contribution to covenant typology in the Scriptures. It creates expectations of a new covenant that will be distinct from the old covenant. Yet it also hints at continuity by speaking about familiar elements of the covenant relationship, like God's law and the forgiveness of sins.

When he alludes to Jeremiah 31:31's "new covenant," Jesus is indicating that the new covenant that he inaugurates is the new covenant that Jeremiah was predicting. In Hebrews 8-10, one sees further reflection on the fulfillment of Jeremiah 31:31-34. Jeremiah speaks about forgiveness of sin in connection with the new covenant and so does Jesus at the Last Supper. Jeremiah does not indicate anything specific about that forgiveness, while Jesus connects that forgiveness with his sacrificial death (Matthew 26:28). Jesus' words also reveal the blood of the covenant that will be associated with the new covenant. It will be his blood.

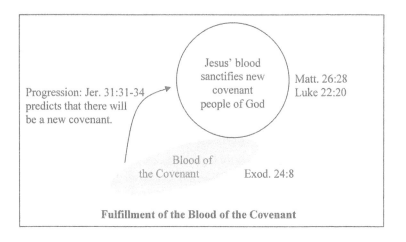

Fulfillment of the Blood of the Covenant

At the Last Supper, Jesus reveals that the new covenant predicted by Jeremiah has finally come. He reveals that this new covenant will be like the old in that God's people will be sanctified with blood of the covenant, as they once were at Mount Sinai. In true typological fashion, it will also be radically different, because the new blood of the covenant has a fullness that was not present in the Old Testament shadow. The true blood of the covenant will not come from an animal, but from the sacrificial death of the Christ.

So, what can we now say about Jesus' words at the Last Supper? When Jesus speaks about his blood as "blood of the covenant" (Matthew and Mark) or of the cup as representing "the new covenant in my blood" (Luke), he would appear to mean at least three things. (1) In light of Jesus' emphasis upon his fulfillment of the Old Testament (Luke 24:44), he means that his blood is the new blood of the covenant that fulfills the blood of the covenant that was sprinkled on God's people at Mount Sinai. (2) In light of this fulfillment, Jesus sees the shedding of his blood as part of the establishment of a new covenant between God and his people. (3) Jesus' blood sanctifies the new covenant people of God so that they become a "royal priesthood" and a "holy nation" (Exodus 19:6 in 1 Peter 2:9).

When we remember Jesus' words about his blood, we are recalling that his blood established the new covenant people of God, of which all Christians are a part. We are also remembering that his blood sanctified us, or made us holy, when we became Christians. Peter appears to add something further here. He adds that it is the Spirit who sanctifies us with the blood of Jesus (1 Peter 1:2). More importantly, he appears to call us to reflect further on the commitment to obedience that accompanied the ratification of the first covenant (Exodus 24:7). He says that our sanctification by the sprinkled blood of Jesus is similarly a sanctification "unto obedience" (1 Peter 1:2). Consequently, when we reflect on Jesus' blood of the covenant and our sanctification, we should also reflect on the association between covenant and obedience to God's words. Becoming part of the covenant people of God means accepting the call to strive to live as God's holy people ought to live, namely, in accordance with God's words as revealed in the Scriptures.[16]

The Last Supper and the Fulfillment of the Passover

The third typology to which Jesus alludes at the Last Supper has to do with the Passover. In some ways, this typology is the most obvious one to look for in the Last Supper. After all, so many aspects of Jesus' death fulfill Scripture. One would expect that the timing of his death at Passover time would fulfill the Scriptures as well. It is interesting that interpreters often do not see much of a connection between the words of Jesus at the Last Supper and the Passover. As we will see in the next chapter, the Gospel of John appears to see a connection between them and describes the death of Jesus in ways that emphasize its connection to the Passover. In this section, we will look first at the two most obvious connections between the words of Jesus at the Last Supper and the Passover. These connections involve the ritual of the bread and the command to celebrate the Lord's Supper in remembrance of him.

Next, the second step will be to look at the deeper connection between the death of Jesus and the Passover. We will see how the Passover is the sacrifice that prefigures the saving death of Jesus. The Passover celebrates salvation. Through the Passover, God delivered his people from death and from slavery in Egypt. Similarly, Jesus' death saves believers from sin, death, and slavery. The saving significance of Jesus' death is evident in Matthew, Mark, Luke, and Acts. Jesus' words at the Last Supper are an important contributor to the Gospels' presentation of the saving death of Jesus. By associating his death with the Passover, Jesus emphasizes that his death is the new saving event that believers are supposed to celebrate until he comes.

"This Is My Body, Which Is Given for You"

First, what does Jesus say at the Last Supper that alludes to the Passover? We have talked a lot in this chapter about Jesus' words about his blood in relation to various sacrifices. We now need to look more closely at his words about his body. In the first place, we are going to see that the ritual of the bread points to a connection between Jesus' body and the Passover sacrifice. In a Passover setting, Jesus institutes the ritual of the bread. Luke 22:19 says, "And after he took bread and gave thanks, he broke it and gave it to them, saying, 'This is my body, which is given for you; do this in remembrance of me.'" In Matthew 26:26, Jesus says, "Take, eat; this is my body" (see also Mark 14:22). In this case, it is Luke that provides the key phrase that probably has sacrificial significance.

Jesus connects his body to the bread and gives it to the disciples to eat. Jesus describes his body as "given for you." Jesus says something very similar about his flesh in John 6:51. John 6:51 has significant sacrificial overtones, which we will look at in the next chapter. It would be reasonable to suspect that "given for you" has some relationship to the sacrifices, because of the sacrificial language that Jesus uses with respect to his blood.

When we look at the Old Testament, we only find one instance where someone "gives" a sacrifice. Ordinarily, the Old Testament speaks about someone offering a sacrifice instead of giving it. David is the only one who speaks about giving a sacrifice to the Lord in Psalm 51:16. One has to look a bit further for a stronger connection between "giving" and sacrifices in the Old Testament. As we have seen several times before, it may be possible to detect a stronger link if we compare Jesus' words in Greek to the Greek of the Septuagint translation. A stronger link occurs not with the verb "give," but with the related noun "gift." In the Septuagint, an animal that the worshiper brings to the Tabernacle or Temple for sacrifice is often called a "gift" (*dōron*) (for examples, see Leviticus 1:2, 3, 10, 14). As one would suspect from the English translation, "gift" (*dōron*) is related to the Greek verb translated "give" in Jesus' phrase "given for you."

The Old Testament parallels are helpful. They support the possibility that Jesus' words might allude to giving a sacrifice. One finds the best evidence that Jesus' words have a sacrificial connection in the Gospel of Luke itself. In Luke 2:24, Jesus' parents go to Jerusalem "to give a sacrifice." Jesus uses the same Greek verb in Luke 22:19, when he speaks about himself as "given for you." The immediate context of Luke 22:19 also supports the sacrificial significance of "given for you." In 22:20, Jesus speaks about his blood using sacrificial language, as we saw earlier in this chapter.

In light of this evidence, it seems likely that "given for you" provides another instance where Jesus is speaking about his death using sacrificial language. By itself, it is not language that one would associate with any particular type of sacrifice. If there is a pointer here to a specific sacrifice, it lies in Jesus' symbolism. The bread represents his body. According to the symbolism, eating the bread represents eating his body. God's people eat the body of the Passover sacrifice, while they do not eat the body of the sin offering or the guilt offering (Leviticus 6:26, 7:7).

Given the Passover setting of the Last Supper, these words would tend to recall the Passover sacrifice that the disciples had just eaten. Luke brings out the Passover setting even more clearly than Matthew and Mark. In Luke 22:15, Jesus speaks about desiring to "eat the Passover" with his disciples before he suffers. Unleavened bread is an essential part of the Passover (Exodus 12:8). Later Jewish sources, like the Mishnah, speak about the place of wine in celebrations of the Passover. Luke specifically mentions two cups of wine at the Last Supper (22:17, 20). Even though it is not specifically mentioned, Jesus' disciples would have been eating their Passover sacrifice at the Last Supper.

According to Exodus 12:27, the Passover meal provides an opportunity for instruction, especially of the children. In Exodus 12:27, Moses tells the parents what they are to teach their children about the meaning of the Passover sacrifice. In Exodus 13:8-9, Moses does the same thing with respect to the unleavened bread at Passover time. As the celebration of the Passover evolved, the instruction element developed to the point where various aspects of the Passover meal are interpreted during the course of the meal. It is hard to know how much teaching was done at Passover meals in Jesus' day, but the point is that God instituted the Passover as a time for instruction. Passover has a significance that God's people are supposed to know and teach at Passover time.

In a Passover context, then, instruction about the meaning of the Passover is normal and expected. Jesus' new teaching goes beyond the expected in that he begins to teach about his body and his blood. He speaks about them both in sacrificial language. He tells his disciples to partake of bread and wine that represent his body and blood. He is the new sacrifice and they are supposed to eat it, symbolically, by eating the bread. It seems reasonable to conclude that Jesus is alluding to a relationship between his sacrificial death and the Passover sacrifice. In light of his other teaching about fulfillment of the Old Testament, Jesus probably means to indicate that his death fulfills the Passover. We will look at the difficulty introduced by the connection between wine and blood, when we look at John 6 in the next chapter.

"Do This in Remembrance of Me"

Jesus' words about his body provide a second parallel to the Passover. Recall Luke 22:19, which says, "This is my body, which is given for you; do this in remembrance of me." What does Jesus mean when he says, "Do this in remembrance of me"? How is this phrase related to the Passover? The clause occurs for the first time with reference to the bread (Luke 22:19, 1 Corinthians 11:24). According to 1 Corinthians 11:24-25, Jesus says "do this in remembrance of me" twice, with respect to both the bread and the cup. The first key word here is the pronoun "this." What does "this" refer back to? In this case, it appears to refer back to one specific action or to the whole ritual concerning the bread.[17] It would probably be a mistake to limit the antecedent of "this" to eating the bread or to saying the words concerning the bread. In either of those cases, "eat this" or "say this" would have been clearer than "do this." Rather, it probably refers back to the whole ritual, including the blessing, breaking the bread, giving it to the disciples, and saying the words about the bread.[18] Consequently, when Jesus commands his disciples to "do this," he is commanding them to engage in the whole ritual of the bread. In Luke 22:20, Jesus does not repeat the command to "do this" with reference to the cup, but the close association between the bread and the cup would tend to imply that Jesus meant for his disciples to do both. According to Paul, Jesus commanded his disciples to engage in the ritual of the bread and then repeated the same command with reference to the ritual of the cup (1 Corinthians 11:24-25).

The second key word in Jesus' command is "remembrance." When Jesus says, "do this in remembrance of me," he is still with his disciples. "Remembrance" involves looking back on something in the past. Therefore, Jesus' command to "do this in remembrance" only makes sense if he is instituting a ritual that he expects to be repeated in the future.[19] Paul's account of Jesus' words makes it even clearer that Jesus is looking into the future. With respect to the cup, Jesus says, "Do this, as often as you are drinking it, in remembrance of me" (1 Corinthians 11:25). The addition of "as often as you are drinking it" shows that Jesus was already anticipating their future celebrations of the Last Supper.

Jesus' disciples are supposed to do this in remembrance "of me." Since Jesus' words over the bread and the cup focus on his sacrificial death, Jesus is calling his disciples to celebrate the ritual of the bread and the cup specifically in remembrance of his death. Paul supports this point in 1 Corinthians 11:26, which immediately follows his account of the Last Supper. He says, "For as often as you are eating this bread and drinking this cup, you are proclaiming the Lord's death until he comes" (11:26). Paul correctly identifies the focus of the ritual as "the Lord's death." After Jesus' death, Paul calls the ritual the "Lord's Supper" (1 Corinthians 11:20).

Why does Paul call it the "Lord's Supper"? "Lord's Supper" likely means that the Lord himself instituted or commanded his disciples to celebrate this supper. After all, Paul reports that the Lord commanded his disciples to "do this" and that he received instructions about the Lord's Supper "from the Lord" (1 Corinthians 11:23-25). Otherwise, it could indicate that the Lord's Supper is dedicated to the Lord or in his honor.[20] Perhaps both of these are relevant.

In light of our understanding of "do this in remembrance of me," we can now look at how this command relates to the Passover. According to Luke 22, Jesus speaks these words in a Passover context. In Exodus 12, God tells Moses how to keep the Passover (12:1-13). God then commands his people to celebrate the Passover and the related Feast of Unleavened Bread as a yearly feast (12:14-20). They must do this every year, for the celebration of the Passover is a "lasting ordinance" (Exodus 12:14). We see here the first parallels or similarities to the Last Supper. Jesus shows his disciples how to celebrate the Lord's Supper and then he commands them to celebrate it in his memory. Paul clearly has the expectation that believers will be celebrating the Lord's Supper until Jesus comes back (1 Corinthians 11:26). It, too, is a lasting ordinance.

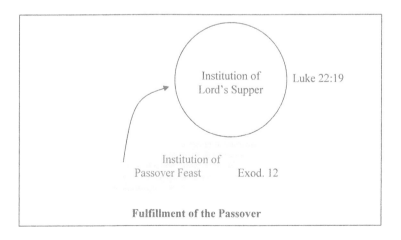

Institution of
Lord's Supper

Luke 22:19

Institution of
Passover Feast   Exod. 12

Fulfillment of the Passover

Exodus 12:14 also sounds similar to "do this in remembrance of me," because it tells God's people that the yearly celebration of Passover will be a "memorial" or a "day of remembrance" (New Revised Standard Version).[21] It is supposed to remind God's people of the day on which God brought them out of Egypt (12:17). In Exodus 13:3, Moses commands God's people to remember the day on which they came out of Egypt. The Feast of Unleavened Bread will be a reminder to them of the Exodus from Egypt (13:9). So, God institutes the Passover, in association with the Feast of Unleavened Bread, as a reminder to God's people of the great day of their salvation or deliverance from slavery in Egypt. Corresponding to this, Jesus institutes the Lord's Supper as a reminder to God's people of his death, which secures their ultimate salvation.[22]

How Jesus' Sacrifice Fulfills the Passover in Matthew, Mark, Luke, and Acts

By instituting the Lord's Supper at a Passover meal, Jesus suggests an association between his death and the Passover. Eating bread and drinking wine are normal parts of a Passover meal. Jesus takes these and interprets them with reference to his sacrificial death. His death is the great saving event that fulfills the Passover. It is hard to avoid the implication that Jesus' death fulfills the Passover lamb in addition to the other sacrifices mentioned earlier. Matthew, Mark, and Luke do not hit on this fulfillment directly. Paul says, "Christ our Passover lamb has been sacrificed" (1 Corinthians 5:9). John makes the most out of Christ's fulfillment of the Passover, which will be the subject of the next chapter.

The fulfillment of the Passover may be more relevant to Matthew, Mark, and Luke than it appears on the surface. In Matthew, the name "Jesus" anticipates that Jesus "will save his people from their sins" (1:21). The Lord's Supper in Matthew connects the pouring out of the blood of Jesus to the "forgiveness of sins" (26:28). Apparently, Jesus saves his people from their sins by dying a sacrificial death.

Luke is not as direct, but he does provide two significant hints that he connects the death of Jesus to the salvation of believers. At the Last Supper, Jesus says that his body is "given for you" and his blood is "poured out for you" (Luke 22:19-20). His death is for their benefit. Later, Acts spells out one of the benefits secured by his blood. Jesus' blood "purchased" his people (20:28). This purchase language presents Jesus' blood as the price that freed his people from bondage. In other words, it points to the saving power and significance of the blood of Jesus. The language of purchase connects with the New Testament theme of redemption from bondage to sin. Redemption from bondage to sin through the blood of Jesus fulfills the Passover, which is the primary redemptive event in the Old Testament. At the time of the Passover, God purchased his people from Pharaoh and the Egyptians (Exodus 15:16, Deuteronomy 32:6). Of course, this was not a traditional purchase, because Pharaoh and the Egyptians did not receive any money or other benefit in the purchase. We will look further at this in the next chapter.

Mark's main statement about the death of Jesus occurs in Mark 10:45, which says that the Son of Man came to "give his life as a ransom for many." This statement shares "for many" with Jesus' words about the blood at the Last Supper (14:24). It occurs in Matthew 20:28 as well. The meaning of Jesus' ransom saying ("give his life as a ransom for many") is often debated. The Old Testament speaks several times about giving a ransom for someone's life or redeeming someone's life (for example, Exodus 21:30, Numbers 35:31, Psalm 34:22). Earlier in Mark, Jesus asks what someone could give in return for his life (8:37). In light of these verses, it appears likely that Jesus' ransom saying provides an answer for his question. Although a person cannot offer a fit ransom for his life, Jesus has come to offer his life as a fit ransom in exchange for the lives of many. Why do the lives of many need to be ransomed from death? The answer is not given, but perhaps it is implied. If "for many" alludes to Isaiah 53 as it does in Jesus' words about his blood, then sin would be the likely answer. The Servant of Isaiah 53 bears the sins of many (53:12). As a result, Jesus gives his life as the ransom that frees many from the penalty of death due to their sins. The ransom saying points to the saving significance of the death of Jesus.

We have now seen that Matthew, Mark, and Luke all present the death of Jesus as having significance for the salvation of God's people. It is therefore not surprising that Jesus died at Passover time. Nor is it surprising that Jesus would allude to the Passover in his words at the Last Supper. The Passover is a vital aspect of the Exodus from Egypt. The Passover is the most important event in the Old Testament where God steps in to save his people from their oppressors. The Old Testament tells us this by repeatedly recalling the Exodus and predicting a new Exodus for God's people.

According to Matthew, Mark, and Luke, Jesus' death saves believers from sin and death. This connects with one aspect of the Passover (Exodus 12). On the night of the Passover, the Lord passed through Egypt and killed the first-born. He passed over the homes that were marked with the blood of the Passover sacrifice. Similarly, Jesus' blood saves his people from God's judgment on sin, which is death. He has come to bring about the ultimate and true Passover and Exodus. As the antitype to the Passover sacrifice, his blood provides eternal salvation from death and sin, which means eternal life for all those who believe. We will return to this in the next chapter.

As we have seen, Jesus' death is the climactic saving event that outshines even the Passover and the Exodus in its significance for the salvation of God's people. Therefore,

Jesus commands believers to remember and celebrate his saving death through the Lord's Supper. The Gospel of John develops Jesus' fulfillment of the Passover much more clearly than Matthew, Mark, and Luke do. Jesus' words at the Last Supper in Matthew, Mark, and Luke already anticipate John's fuller development of this theme. We celebrate the fulfillment of the Passover whenever we celebrate the Lord's Supper. Even as we do so, we realize that our redemption is not complete yet. We are still awaiting the redemption of our bodies (Romans 8:23) and our complete deliverance from the powers of this world. At the Last Supper, Jesus himself points forward to a day when we will celebrate the final and complete fulfillment of the Passover in the kingdom of God (Luke 22:15-16).

Synthesis and Conclusion

Jesus appears to be alluding to three related Old Testament typologies in his words at the Last Supper. They are the sacrifices of atonement, the blood of the covenant, and the Passover. The unifying thread that ties all three together is salvation from sin and death. As the true sacrifice of atonement, his blood makes atonement for believers' sins, which results in forgiveness of sins and being reconciled to God. His blood is blood of the new covenant that sanctifies believers so that they become God's holy people. Sanctification cannot take place without atonement for sins, because becoming God's holy people requires reconciliation to God to overcome the alienation caused by sin. Why do people need atonement for sin and sanctification?

According to the New Testament, those who belong to the world are in bondage to sin and the devil. They sin and they will face God's judgment and wrath. The penalty for sin is death. In order to deliver people from death due to sin, Jesus died at Passover time as the ultimate and final sacrifice.

When people believe in Jesus, they receive the benefits of his sacrificial death for them, including atonement and sanctification. As a result, they are God's holy people, whom he has saved from judgment and death. Jesus' blood, like the blood of the Passover sacrifice, saves the new covenant people of God from his wrath. Since God sanctified his people, they now belong to God and are his servants. They are no longer in bondage to sin and the devil.

If I have described the big picture correctly, then Jesus' words at the Last Supper point to the saving significance of his sacrificial death. At the moment of our conversion, his blood makes atonement for our sins and sanctifies us. In doing so, his blood saves us from sin and death. When the Last Supper/Lord's Supper is properly taught and celebrated, it should lead to a sense of profound gratitude and loving praise. Jesus truly does save his people from their sins. He does so through his own blood, poured out for many, for the forgiveness of sins. Next, we turn to the Gospel of John and his version of the big picture of our salvation through the Lamb of God who takes away the sin of the world. John's big picture contains many of the elements mentioned above, so we will be able to see how John teaches us about salvation through the body and blood of Jesus.

Chapter 4

The Fulfillment of the Passover in the Gospel of John

—⁊⁊⁊—

Exalus

The Exodus from Egypt is the major saving event of the Old Testament. God initially reveals its significance by requiring his people to recall this event every year at Passover and the Feast of Unleavened Bread. The Psalms reveal its significance by recalling God's great deliverance of his people at the time of the Exodus. The prophets reveal its significance by recalling the Exodus and using it as a pattern to describe God's anticipated deliverance of his people. When Jesus comes proclaiming the fulfillment of the Old Testament expectations, he further confirms the significance of the Exodus by showing how it provides the pattern for an even greater saving event, his saving death.

Within the story of the Exodus, the Passover plays a central role. The Passover is the final plague that causes Pharaoh to relent and let God's people go. It is central to the redemption of God's people from slavery in Egypt under Pharaoh. The Passover leads to freedom from bondage. It represents victory over Pharaoh and his power. A closer look at the Passover also reveals that it contains another main emphasis. The Passover celebrates a night when God

85

passed over those who completed the Passover sacrifice and brought death to the firstborn sons of those who did not. The two main emphases of the Passover, then, are freedom from bondage and deliverance from death. As we will see below, both of these main emphases are closely related to the significance of the Passover sacrifice.

The Gospel of John contains both of the main emphases of the Passover. Jesus, the Lamb of God, dies a sacrificial death at Passover time. Believers must eat the flesh and drink the blood of the Lamb of God. Receiving the flesh and blood of Jesus frees believers from slavery to sin and the devil. It also delivers believers from death. Their freedom comes about through the Lamb's victory over the devil and his power. Most of these points emerge directly from Jesus' own teaching in the Gospel of John. More than anywhere else in the Gospels, John is the place in which Jesus reveals how he fulfills the Passover. The Passover was a great saving event that points to an even greater saving event, the saving death of Christ. In John 5:46, Jesus claims, "Moses wrote about me." The most significant way in which Moses wrote about Jesus probably has to do with the Passover and its fulfillment.

In order to appreciate John's Passover typology, we will first look more closely at the Passover and especially the significance of the Passover sacrifice. Then we will look at the passages in the Gospel of John that contribute to the fulfillment of the Passover. As we proceed in this way, we will note how careful attention to the type, the Passover, helps us to avoid some theological pitfalls in our interpretation of the redeeming death of Jesus.

The Passover

Jesus and his apostles would probably have interpreted the Passover as part of the five books of Moses and with the help of the Old Testament as a whole. Therefore, I will proceed to interpret it within the larger context of the books of Moses. From time to time, we will also look beyond the books of Moses to see how other parts of the Old Testament shed light on the interpretation of the Passover. My understanding of the New Testament's teaching about the Passover's fulfillment will also shape my treatment of the Passover. This shaping is necessary, because my goal is to show the relationship between type and antitype. In other words, I am trying to approximate an interpretation of the Passover that would make sense to Jesus and his apostles. I am also trying to focus on those elements that are most relevant to the New Testament's teaching about the fulfillment of the Passover. As I mentioned earlier, the Passover has two emphases, namely, freedom from bondage and deliverance from death. We will look first at Israel's bondage and the non-traditional nature of God's redemption of Israel. Then, we will see how redemption from bondage and deliverance from death are related to the significance of the Passover sacrifice.

The Passover Redeems Israel from Bondage to Pharaoh and the Egyptians

God says that he has come to redeem his people from bondage in Egypt (Exodus 6:6). Redemption usually involves paying money to free a slave from bondage. God's redemption of Israel from Pharaoh and the Egyptians is not a traditional redemption. God does not pay Pharaoh anything. Careful attention to this point prepares us to understand the teaching of the New Testament about redemption from bondage to sin and the devil. Rather than pay Pharaoh, God proclaims that Israel is his firstborn son. If Pharaoh will not let Israel go, then God will kill Pharaoh's firstborn son (Exodus 4:22-23). Killing the firstborn of Egypt, including Pharaoh's firstborn son, is the climactic plague that causes

Pharaoh to release Israel from slavery. These are the essential points that establish a connection between Passover and redemption from slavery. As we examine these points, we will see their importance for our understanding of Passover and for a proper approach to Passover typology.

The Lord reveals the central place of the Passover to Moses even before Moses speaks to Pharaoh for the first time. In Exodus 4:22-23, God says, "Then you shall say to Pharaoh, 'Thus says the LORD, "Israel is My son, My firstborn. So I said to you, 'Let My son go that he may serve Me'; but you have refused to let him go. Behold, I will kill your son, your firstborn"'" (NASB). These verses, along with Exodus 4:21, predict the climax of Moses' confrontation with Pharaoh. They are very important verses, because the Lord reveals the nature of his relationship to his people. Israel is his firstborn son. Exodus 4:22-23 is the first time in the Old Testament where God calls Israel his son. Israel is his firstborn son due to God's gracious election and adoption of Israel as his own, which results in a covenant relationship between them that goes back to Abraham (Exodus 2:24, 19:5-6; Deuteronomy 14:1-2).[1]

If Israel is his firstborn son, then God is the Father who has come to redeem his son from bondage. One finds evidence for this point later in the Old Testament. According to Deuteronomy 32:6, the Lord is the Father who bought Israel, which refers back to the Exodus (Exodus 15:16). In Isaiah 63:16, God is his people's Father and Redeemer, which he showed at the time of the Exodus. Psalm 74:2 refers back to the Exodus again, as the time when God purchased and redeemed his people. By identifying God as the redeeming Father, these verses present God in a role that is comparable to the kinsman redeemer of Leviticus 25:47-55. If a poor Israelite sells himself into service as a hired man, one of his blood relatives may redeem him by paying for his redemption (25:48-49). No Israelite should sell himself into full slavery again, because God delivered his people from slavery in Egypt to serve him (25:55). At the time of the Exodus, God identifies himself as Israel's Father. He comes as Israel's close kinsman to redeem Israel from bondage in Egypt.

The redeeming and purchasing language in the verses above appears to refer to a business transaction between the Lord and Pharaoh. Of course, one finds no such transaction anywhere in Exodus. Instead, God redeems his people from bondage without paying any redemption money. After referring to his covenant relationship with his people (Exodus 6:5), the Lord identifies freedom from bondage and redemption as his goal (6:6). He says, "Therefore, say to the Israelites: 'I am the LORD, and I will bring you out from under the yoke of the Egyptians. I will free you from being slaves to them, and I will redeem you with an outstretched arm and with mighty acts of judgment'" (NIV). Notice that there is no mention of payment of money. God is going to redeem his people through his powerful arm and acts of judgment. This sounds more like a rescue operation than a business deal.

Why all of the redemption and purchasing language if Pharaoh does not get paid? First, the language emphasizes God's goal in his dealings with Pharaoh. Beginning with Exodus 4:23, quoted above, God repeatedly tells Pharaoh to let his people go so that they may "serve" him (7:16, 8:1, etc.). The people later recall that in Egypt they were serving the Egyptians (Exodus 14:12). Leviticus 25:55 affirms that God redeemed his people so that they could be his servants rather than be slaves to Pharaoh and the Egyptians. As redeeming Father, God has come to claim his people as his own first-born son and his servants. God later confirms their special position as his own holy people when he speaks about the covenant at Mount Sinai (Exodus 19:5-6). God's goal, then, is nothing less than a transfer of ownership. He intends to redeem his people from slavery to Pharaoh and at the same time purchase them for himself. Then, they may freely serve him as his own holy people.

Second, God intends to redeem his people without money, because Pharaoh and the Egyptians unjustly enslaved God's people in the first place. The Lord says in Isaiah 52:3, "You were sold for nothing, and without money you will be redeemed" (NIV). Isaiah 52:4 then mentions slavery in Egypt as an example of this. Exodus 1:8-14 shows how the Egyptians followed the lead of Pharaoh in forcing the Israelites into slavery. Exodus 1:13 and 6:5 stress their enslavement by the Egyptians. God never sold them into bondage. Therefore, when God comes to redeem his people, he comes to break the yoke of slavery rather than to redeem them with money. This is an important point. When some Church Fathers were writing about Christ's redemption of his people, they failed to take into account that God did not pay Pharaoh. If God did not pay Pharaoh at the time of the Passover, then one would not expect God to pay the devil when Jesus fulfills the Passover.

When God redeems his people, he forces Pharaoh to release them through his "mighty acts of judgment" (Exodus 6:6). The acts of judgment take the form of ten plagues. They reveal his power to Pharaoh (9:14-16). God's final judgment on Egypt occurs during the night after the Passover sacrifice. It is a plague that brings death to the firstborn sons and firstborn animals of Egypt. After this plague, Pharaoh finally relents and lets God's people go so that they might serve him (12:31). God's people leave Egypt never to return to bondage there. Pharaoh no longer owns God's people; they belong to God. In this section, we have seen that one central aspect of Passover is freedom from slavery to Pharaoh and the Egyptians.

The Passover Sacrifice Sanctifies Servants for God and Delivers Them from Death

Passover celebrates an ominous event in the history of God's people. On the night of the final plague, God protects the firstborn of Israel through the institution of the Passover sacrifice. On closer inspection, the Passover sacrifice does more than protect the firstborn sons from death. The Passover sacrifice prepares servants for God by sanctifying the firstborn sons of Israel. Consequently, the firstborn sons belong to God and are his servants. The Passover sacrifice sets them apart from the firstborn of Egypt. The sanctifying Passover sacrifice also delivers the firstborn sons from God's judgment, because it reconciles the firstborn to God by making atonement for their sins. They are saved from death by the blood of the Passover sacrifice. The sanctification and salvation of the firstborn sons is likely symbolic. As we will see below, it probably symbolizes God's deeper purpose, the redemption of Israel to serve him as his "kingdom of priests" (Exodus 19:6). In this section, we will look at the evidence for these points and their significance for our understanding of the Passover sacrifice.

In the case of the previous plagues, God spared Israel from harm. In the case of the Passover, deliverance is not automatic for Israel. It depends on obeying God's regulations for the Passover sacrifice. To understand the significance of the Passover sacrifice, it helps to compare it with other Old Testament sacrifices. The various rules for the Passover sacrifice resemble those for a thanksgiving peace offering more than they resemble the rules for any other sacrifice (Leviticus 7:11-14). For instance, in both cases, the sacrifice is eaten with at least some unleavened bread and must be eaten on the same day. The similarity is probably not coincidental. Thanksgiving peace offerings are often associated with thanksgiving for deliverance, including deliverance from enemies and death (Psalm 56:12-13).[2] We see evidence here of God's special design of the Passover.

God institutes a special sacrifice that resembles a thanksgiving peace offering, because he means for the Passover sacrifice to do two things. First, it delivers his people from slavery and death. Second, the yearly Passover sacrifice is an occasion for thanksgiving in memory of deliverance from slavery and death. It appears, then, that God designed the Passover to be a yearly time of thanksgiving for deliverance. That is why God closely associates the first Passover and subsequent celebrations of the Passover in his words to Moses in Exodus 12. The yearly celebration of deliverance includes the Passover sacrifice, which resembles a thanksgiving peace offering. The Passover is eaten with unleavened bread, which recalls their hasty departure from Egypt (Exodus 12:39). It is also eaten with "bitter herbs," which are a reminder of the bitterness of slavery in Egypt (Exodus 12:8, 1:14). From the very first, two central aspects of the Passover are deliverance and yearly thanksgiving for deliverance.

In the previous section, we saw that God uses the plague of death to deliver Israel from slavery in Egypt. God chooses to use the Passover sacrifice to protect his people from this plague. Why does he choose the Passover sacrifice? What does it accomplish? How does it deliver the firstborn sons from death? Although one could find various answers to these questions in the works of modern interpreters, the best answers to these questions emerge from careful consideration of Numbers 3:13, 8:17 along with Exodus 13:2, 11-16. God says, "For all the firstborn are Mine; on the day that I struck down all the firstborn in the land of Egypt, I sanctified to Myself all of the firstborn in Israel, from man to beast" (Numbers 3:13, NASB). This verse identifies a third central aspect of the Passover, namely, the sanctification of the firstborn sons. By examining the sanctification of the firstborn sons, we will arrive at the answers to our three questions.

How did God sanctify the firstborn sons? The Passover sacrifice seems to be the likely answer. We see this when we compare it to the ordination ram that is part of the sanctification of the priests in Exodus 29 and Leviticus 8. We looked briefly at the ordination ram in the last chapter in relation to the covenant sacrifices of Exodus 24. We will now compare it to the Passover sacrifice. The ordination ram, like the Passover sacrifice, corresponds in significant ways to a thanksgiving peace offering. All of these are eaten along with bread on the same day as the sacrifice. Unleavened bread appears to be more central in the case of the Passover and the ordination ram (Exodus 12:8; 29:23, 32). The Passover sacrifice and ordination ram differ markedly from a thanksgiving peace offering in that both include special instructions concerning the blood. The blood of the ordination ram was applied to the priests and their garments to sanctify them or make them holy (Exodus 29:21). The blood of the Passover sacrifice was poured out and some of it was applied to the sides and top of the doorway of the house (Exodus 12:7). It is likely that the blood of the Passover sacrifice sanctified all of the firstborn sons and animals in the house.[3] This is why God says that he sanctified Israel's firstborn sons and animals when he struck the firstborn of the Egyptians. God sanctified them through the blood of the Passover sacrifice. Their sanctification set them apart from the firstborn of the Egyptians. As was the case with earlier plagues (Exodus 8:22-23), the Passover sacrifice indicates a separation between God's people and Pharaoh's people.

In order to appreciate the significance of the analogy between the Passover sacrifice and the ordination ram, we need to understand how the sanctification of the priests relates to the sanctification of Israel as a whole. To be a holy or sanctified person means to be "given to God" or "dedicated to the service of God."[4] Among all of Israel, the priests are at the highest level of holiness. Their lives are dedicated to serving God to the greatest extent. To a lesser degree, all of Israel is holy. When Moses sprinkles them with the blood of the covenant, Israel is sanctified and becomes a "kingdom of priests and a holy nation" (Exodus 19:6, 24:8). As God's priestly people, they serve God in accordance with the Law of Moses (Leviticus 25:55). In both cases, sanctification requires sacrifice and the application of blood.

If the sanctification of the firstborn sons and animals is like these sanctifications, then we would expect to find out that they are given to God and what it means for them to be given to God. As we have seen already, Numbers 3:13 says that the firstborn belong to God. In the case of the firstborn animals, Exodus 13:12-15 says that this generally means that they are to be devoted to the Lord and sacrificed. The firstborn sons, on the other hand, belong to the Lord as well and must be redeemed (13:15). Their redemption is to be a continual reminder of the first Passover (13:15). We eventually learn about the redemption of the firstborn sons in Numbers 3 and 8. God tells Moses to offer the Levites to him to redeem the firstborn sons. The Levites are wholly given to God to serve Aaron and the Tabernacle (Numbers 8:16, 19). We conclude from this that God's sanctification of the firstborn sons is special. It transcends the sanctification of the ordinary Israelite, because only the Levites are acceptable as the equivalent to the firstborn sons. The Levites are right below the priests in terms of their level of holiness. This means that their lives are dedicated or given to the Lord's service in a special way, similar to the priests.

Why is it so important to understand the connection between the Passover sacrifice and sanctification of the firstborn? The Passover sacrifice and the sanctification of the firstborn are thoroughly in line with God's primary goal at the time of the Exodus. God aims to free his people so that they might be his servants. Starting in Exodus 4:22-23, God asks Pharaoh to release Israel, his firstborn son, so that his son might serve him. He clarifies the nature of the service that he wants from Israel in terms of offering sacrifices to him in the wilderness (5:3, 7:16, etc.). Through the Passover sacrifice, God sanctifies the firstborn sons for his service. As a result, they already belong to God and his service even before they leave Egypt. They no longer belong to Pharaoh and his service. They are God's servants now. The later redemption of the firstborn sons by the Levites reinforces the point. The Levites are special servants of God, who serve under Aaron at the Tabernacle. Therefore, through the Passover sacrifice, God sanctifies servants for his service.

We can now appreciate that the sanctification of the firstborn sons points to God's primary goal at the time of the Passover. He sanctifies the firstborn sons, because they represent Israel. Israel is his firstborn son. Before leaving Egypt, God already transfers ownership of the firstborn sons to himself through the Passover sacrifice. He then strikes the firstborn sons of Egypt with death to free his firstborn son, Israel, from bondage to Pharaoh and the Egyptians so that Israel can serve him as his own holy people. His firstborn son, Israel, rightly belongs to him and his service. God intends to free Israel and then make a covenant with them, as Exodus 6:6-7 shows. At Mount Sinai, in the wilderness, Israel later becomes God's "kingdom of priests" and "holy nation" through the sanctifying blood of the covenant (Exodus 19:6, 24:3-8). As his kingdom of priests, they are all servants of God and therefore do not belong in slavery to any other master (Leviticus 25:47-55).

We can now appreciate why God associates the Passover sacrifice with sanctification. A lingering question remains, however. How does the Passover sacrifice deliver the firstborn sons from death? To answer this question, it is probably important to repeat here a few points from the last chapter's section on the blood of the covenant. The ordination ram for the priests provides an important instance where a special peace offering makes atonement and sanctifies (Exodus 29:33). The Passover sacrifice, which is similar to the ordination ram, probably also makes atonement and sanctifies. Furthermore, it is likely that the Passover sacrifice makes atonement, because sacrifices that sanctify normally make atonement as well. In fact, as we saw in the last chapter, the Law closely relates making atonement, cleansing from sin and impurity, and sanctification when it comes to the benefits of certain Old Testament sacrifices (Leviticus 8:15, 16:18-19). Therefore, if the Passover sacrifice makes atonement and sanctifies, it probably cleanses from sin and impurity as well.[5] This makes good sense. How could one become God's holy servant through sanctification without also being cleansed from sin and reconciled to God through making atonement?

When it comes to delivering the firstborn sons from death, making atonement is more significant than sanctification. Recall that the plague that kills the firstborn sons of Egypt is one of God's "great judgments" on Egypt (Exod 6:6, 7:4). This plague displays the wrath of God on Egypt (Psalm 78:49-51). Therefore, the Passover sacrifice spares the firstborn sons from death due to a plague sent from God (Exod 12:12-13, 23). On some occasions in the Old Testament, God sends a deadly plague to judge his people for serious sin and rebellion against him. Making atonement delivers them from the deadly plague.[6] The Passover lamb's blood prevents the plague from entering homes that have its blood around the doors, because this sacrifice makes atonement for the ones who are inside. As we saw in chapter three, the blood of a sacrifice of atonement makes atonement for the sinner, which means that it reconciles the sinner to God. Those who are reconciled to God have nothing to fear from his judgment or wrath. The blood of the Passover lamb delivers them from death.

As we conclude our consideration of the Passover, we can now summarize central aspects of the Passover. When

God institutes the Passover, he designs it to be a yearly celebration of deliverance. The original Passover delivers God's people from slavery to Pharaoh and the Egyptians. Through the Passover sacrifice, God sanctifies the firstborn sons, who represent God's people as a whole (Exodus 4:22). Due to their sanctification, the firstborn sons belong to God and his service and not to Pharaoh. On Passover night, the blood of the Passover sacrifice also delivers them from death, because it makes atonement for them. While Passover is often associated with freedom from slavery, it is important to notice that Passover includes a strong emphasis on God's judgment. God's ultimate judgment on Pharaoh and Egypt is the plague of death. The only way to avoid the plague is to sacrifice the Passover in accordance with God's Law. Through the blood of the Passover lamb, God's people are safe from his judgment, which is death.

The Fulfillment of the Passover in the Gospel of John

The Passover is obviously significant for the Gospel of John. John contains three Passovers (2:13, 6:4, 12:1), while the other Gospels only contain one. Although it is common for readers to gloss over John's connections to the Passover, our goal is to show that John actually contains a Passover theme of significant proportions. Much of John's Passover theme comes from the words of Jesus. This is important. We often turn to the letters of Paul when we want to study about the theology of the cross. In this section, we will see some rich, but often neglected, passages in the Gospel of John that teach us about the death of Jesus. Those acquainted with Paul's letters will appreciate significant similarities between the teaching of Jesus and the teaching of Paul. Hopefully, we will all find that John contains rich teaching about the death of Jesus, often from Jesus himself.

The Gospel of John contains both of the major emphases of the Passover. On the one hand, God has sent Jesus to free his people from slavery to sin and the devil. In order to do this, Jesus must die as the true Passover lamb. God's people must eat his flesh and drink his blood. His sacrificial death takes away his people's sin, sanctifies them, and saves them from death. As a result, they belong to God, who sets them free from slavery to sin and the devil. In order to see John's Passover theme, it will help us to look first at the bondage of God's people.

Slavery to Sin and the Devil in John 8:31-47

In John 8:31-47, Jesus shows that his listeners are in slavery to sin and to the devil. Although recent interpreters often do not link these verses to John's Passover theme, some Church Fathers, like Melito of Sardis, show how naturally this passage fits with the fulfillment of the Passover. In a second-century Passover sermon, Melito notes the correspondence between slavery to sin and the devil and slavery to the Egyptians and Pharaoh.[7] John 8:31-47 makes an important contribution to John's teaching about the fulfillment of the Passover. Elsewhere in John, Jesus dies at Passover time as the true Passover sacrifice. If so, then one would expect his death to be connected with freeing God's people from slavery. John 8:31-47 fulfills this expectation by providing both the picture of slavery and the way of redemption.

In John 8:31, Jesus is speaking to some new Jewish believers about true faith or true discipleship.[8] He says, "If you remain in my word, you are truly my disciples, and you will know the truth, and the truth will set you free" (8:31-32). In response, they claim that they are children of Abraham and have never experienced slavery to anyone (8:33). Jesus explains his claim, by saying, "Everyone who practices sin is a slave to sin" (8:34). Next, Jesus speaks about redemption again. As a full son and not a slave, he is going to remain in the Father's house forever. As a result, "if the Son should free you, you will be truly free" (8:36). In 8:37, Jesus presents his grounds for claiming that they are still slaves. Although they are Abraham's children, they are seeking to kill him, because they have no place for his word. By the end of the passage, these new believers show that Jesus is right about them. They pick up stones to stone him (8:59).

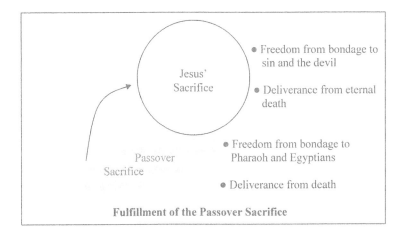

Fulfillment of the Passover Sacrifice

Jesus twice talks about freedom in John 8:31-37. In one case, the truth makes the disciples of Jesus free (8:31-32). In the other case, the Son, Jesus, makes disciples free (8:36). It is important to understand why this is really the same thing. Jesus is essentially teaching these new believers about the difference between fickle belief and true belief. True disciples are those who remain in Jesus' word, which means that they do not forsake the teaching of Jesus. Jesus' word is the truth. The truth sets them free, because they learn the truth about Jesus from his word. Through the truth, they come to know who Jesus truly is and to believe in him based on this true knowledge. True belief in Jesus saves them or sets them free, because Jesus saves or sets free those who truly believe in him. Peter, for instance, shows that he is a true believer in John 6. When others are turning away from Jesus due to his hard teaching, Peter expresses faith in Jesus. He says, "And we have believed and have come to know that you are the holy one of God" (John 6:69). In short, the Gospel of John frequently connects salvation or eternal life to believing in Jesus, because Jesus saves those who truly know him and believe in him. We will see the importance of this point in a few other passages as well.

In John 8:37, Jesus provides his first piece of evidence that these new believers are still in bondage to sin, namely, they are seeking to kill him. Then, in 8:38-44, he makes the case that they are also in bondage to their father, the devil. They are listening to the wrong father. Jesus' words, which he heard from his Father, have no place in them (8:37-38a). Rather, Jesus says, "You are therefore doing what you heard from your father" (8:38b). In the ensuing disagreement, Jesus insists that their actions reveal who their father is. He denies that God is their Father, because they are not listening to the word of Jesus, whom God sent (8:42-43, 47). They belong to their father, the devil, and want to carry out his desires (8:44a).

On closer inspection, we can see the Passover typology in these verses. Jesus claims that God has sent him, just as he once sent Moses (Exodus 3:13-15). Jesus, like Moses, proclaims the good news of freedom to those who are in slavery. He claims that his message comes from his Father. Recall that God first identified himself as his people's Father at the time of the Exodus. Jesus shows that these new believers are in bondage to sin and the devil, while Israel's bondage was to the Egyptians and Pharaoh. Jesus also claims that he is the one who can make them free (8:36). God freed his people at the time of the Exodus. Jesus is greater than Moses. He is also God; his Father sent him to free their people. We see this back in 8:24 and 8:28. Jesus says that he will only save those who believe that "I am" (8:24). "I am" is probably short for "I am the Lord." Although it occurs a few times in Genesis, God frequently repeats this phrase with reference to himself at the time of the Exodus (for instance, Exodus 6:2, 6; 12:12). In 8:28, Jesus claims, "Then you will know that I am," which is very similar to "that you may know that I am the Lord" (Exodus 10:2). The Father has sent Jesus, his divine Son, to redeem their people from slavery to sin and the devil at Passover time.

According to John 8:31-47, then, Jesus is the divine redeemer sent by the Father to redeem their people. Their people are different from the people of the devil, because they hear the word of Jesus and believe in him. The children of the devil reject the word of Jesus and refuse to believe. They are in slavery to sin and the devil (1 John 3:8-10). Jesus, the Son, has come to free the Father's people from slavery. How is he going to do so? As was the case at the time of the Passover, Jesus frees the people of God from the power of sin and the devil through his own Passover sacrifice. As we will see in the next section, eating Jesus' flesh and drinking his blood sanctifies believers so that they become children of God. God's children are rightly his servants rather than servants to the devil. God is their Father and they listen to him (John 8:47). Once they become God's children, the Father and Son protect them from the devil's power (John 10:28-29; 17:12, 15).

Table 3: Summary of Gospel of John Themes as They Relate to Passover		
Gospel of John Theme	**Main Elements**	**Related Passover Emphasis**
Freedom from bondage to sin and the devil	The Father sends Jesus, his divine Son, to redeem their people from slavery to sin and the devil at Passover time. (John 8:31-47)	The Father sends Moses to redeem Israel from slavery to Pharaoh and the Egyptians at Passover time. (Exod. 3:13-15, 12:1-41)
Becoming children of God	Those who eat Jesus' flesh and drink his blood become children of God. They listen to God rather than to the devil. (John 6:56, 8:47)	The Passover sacrifice sanctifies the firstborn sons so that they belong to God and his service. (Num. 3:13)
Deliverance from death	Those who eat Jesus' flesh and drink his blood have eternal life and will never die. (John 6:54, 8:51)	The Passover sacrifice delivers the firstborn sons from death on the night of the Passover. (Exod. 12:12-13)

One of the neglected themes of the New Testament is bondage to sin and the devil. It sounds out of step with contemporary emphases on freedom from all restraints and self-determination. Meditating on bondage and freedom from it provides another dimension to worship at the Lord's Supper and Easter. The world around us is trying to throw off restraints, but is becoming ever deeper in bondage to sin and the devil. Christians are truly free from this bondage and able to practice true righteousness (1John 3: 7-10). We should appreciate our freedom enough to praise God for it and to walk in the ways of righteousness. Remember that God designed the Passover to be a time of thanksgiving for deliverance. Jesus gave us the Lord's Supper as a time for us to be thankful for our deliverance.

Becoming Children of God through the Flesh and Blood of the Lamb

In the Gospel of John, it is quite evident that Jesus frees his people from slavery and delivers them from death. It is not as evident how these two are related. At the heart of both types of deliverance is the sacrificial death of Jesus. In this section, we will see how the sacrificial death of Jesus contributes to the birth and sanctification of the children of God. Becoming children of God is the key to freedom from slavery to the devil and deliverance from death.

According to John, believers become children of God when they are born of God (1:12-13). Later Jesus speaks about being born of the Spirit (3:6, 8). Where does John connect the sacrificial death of Jesus to the birth of the children of God? The most important passage is John 6:51-58. At Passover time (6:4), Jesus speaks about his flesh and blood using words that sound quite similar to his later words at the Last Supper. He says, "The bread which I will give for the life of the world is my flesh" (6:51b). In Luke 22:19, Jesus speaks about his body as "given for you," uses bread to represent his body, and gives it to his disciples to eat. As we saw in the previous chapter, this is sacrificial language.

Jesus gives his flesh for the life of the world when he dies on the cross as the Lamb of God.

After this point, Jesus' teaching becomes more difficult. He says that anyone who does not eat his flesh and drink his blood does not have life, but the one who eats his flesh and drinks his blood has eternal life (6:53-4). The mere thought of eating someone's flesh is difficult enough by itself. Jesus is speaking these words to Jews. God has expressly forbidden them to drink blood, because blood is for making atonement on the altar (Leviticus 17:11). What does Jesus' language mean? The solution to the dilemma is hinted at in John 6:63, which says that the Spirit, not the flesh, gives life. One aspect of the significance of this verse is that it helps to clarify that Jesus is talking in symbolic language rather than actually advocating that one eat human flesh and drink human blood.

John 6:63 provides further help in that it points to the way in which the believer will eat the flesh and drink the blood of Jesus. If it is the Spirit that gives life, then it is likely to be the Spirit that feeds believers with the flesh and blood of Jesus so that they can have life. Twice John speaks about receiving the Spirit in terms of drinking living water (4:10-14, 7:37-39). Likewise, eating Jesus' flesh and drinking his blood involves receiving the benefits of Jesus' flesh and blood. The symbolism is the same as the symbolism of the Lord's Supper. At the Lord's Supper as well, eating the bread/body and drinking the cup/blood points to receiving the benefits of the sacrificial death of Jesus. At the Lord's Supper, Jesus confirms this by describing his body and blood using sacrificial language, as we saw in the last chapter. When believers are born of the Spirit, they receive the benefits of the sacrificial death of Jesus. The language of eating and drinking connects receiving these benefits to the fulfillment of the Passover. When they eat his flesh and drink his blood, believers fulfill the original Passover, including the application of blood and the Passover meal.

Before looking at the benefits of the flesh and blood of Jesus, we need to look at the death of Jesus in John to see how it supports this picture. In John 19:34, we find the only other mention of Jesus' blood in the Gospel of John. When the soldier pierces Jesus' side, blood and water come out. As Jesus is hanging on the cross, we see his body and the pouring out of his blood. John is the only Gospel to mention the piercing of Jesus' side and the blood coming out. At the Lord's Supper, Jesus spoke about the pouring out of his blood. Here we see it. We also see his body, given for us. The unexpected element is the water. In light of the connection between water and Spirit in John, the water probably represents the Spirit, whom Jesus sends to believers to bring to them the benefits of his sacrificial death, his flesh and blood (6:63, 16:7).

What are the benefits of the sacrificial death of Jesus? John 6:48-58 repeatedly emphasizes that receiving the flesh and blood of Jesus gives life and delivers from death. We will look further at this benefit in the next section. John 6:56 is a key verse for us. Jesus says, "The one who eats my flesh and drinks my blood remains in me and I in him" (6:56). The meaning of this language becomes apparent later, especially in John 15:1-6. Remaining in Jesus means remaining in the "true vine" (15:1, 5). In the Old Testament, a vine is a symbol for God's people in several places (for instance, Psalm 80:8-16, Hosea 10:1). Eating Jesus' flesh and drinking his blood unites the believer with Jesus, the true vine. As a branch connected to the true vine, the believer becomes part of the new covenant people of God. In other words, the believer becomes a child of God through eating Jesus' flesh and drinking his blood. This is a second benefit of receiving the flesh and blood of Jesus.

We can now see how John connects the sacrificial death of Jesus to the birth of the children of God. At the time when believers are born of the Spirit, they receive the flesh and blood of Jesus. They become people of God, his children. Since they are God's children, he is their Father and they belong to him rather than to the devil. Revelation, which John also wrote, appears to make the same point when it says that Jesus purchases people for God with his blood (5:9). Peter likewise says that Christ's blood redeems believers from their sinful way of life (1 Peter 1:18). Jesus' blood purchases or redeems them out of bondage when people receive his blood and become children of God. As was the case with Pharaoh, God does not pay the devil or sin when he purchases his people. He sanctifies his people for himself with the blood of Jesus.

How are the benefits of the sacrificial death of Jesus similar to the benefits of the Passover sacrifice? The Passover sacrifice sanctifies the firstborn sons so that they belong to God, their Father, and to his service. At the same time, the Passover anticipates the later sanctification of Israel through the blood of the covenant, because the firstborn sons represent Israel as a whole (Exodus 4:22). It is therefore not surprising that Jesus' words at the Lord's Supper point to his simultaneous fulfillment of both the Passover and the blood of the covenant.

Table 4: Correspondences between Death of Jesus and Passover in Gospel of John		
Elements of the Passover	**The Death of Jesus in John**	**Passover Verse (NASB)**
Passover sacrifice's bones are not to be broken.	Not one of Jesus' bones is broken.	"Nor are you to break any bone of it." (Exod. 12:46b)
Applying the blood of the Passover sacrifice around the doorway of the house.	Drinking the blood of Jesus, which means receiving the benefits of Jesus' sacrifice from the Spirit.	"They shall take some of the blood and put it on the two doorposts and on the lintel of the houses." (Exod. 12:7)
Eating the Passover sacrifice at the time of deliverance from death and slavery in Egypt.	Eating the flesh of Jesus when a person believes in Jesus, receives the Spirit, and is saved from death and slavery to sin.	"They shall eat the flesh that same night." (Exod. 12:8)
The blood of the Passover sacrifice sanctifies the firstborn sons, who represent Israel.	Jesus' blood sanctifies believers when they receive it from the Spirit.	"On the day that I struck down all the firstborn in the land of Egypt, I sanctified to Myself all the firstborn in Israel." (Num. 3:13)

If Jesus' flesh and blood creates children for God through the Spirit and fulfills the Passover and the blood of the covenant, then sanctification should be one of the sacrificial benefits of Jesus' flesh and blood. Peter and the author of Hebrews explicitly make this connection (1 Peter 1:2, Hebrews 10:29). John points to the same thing in his own way in John 17:13-21. Jesus speaks about the distinction between his people and the people of the world. He prays for the Father to keep his disciples from the evil one, the devil (17:15). He then begins to pray for his disciples' sanctification "by the truth," which he identifies as God's word (17:17).

In John 17:19, he prays, "And for them I sanctify myself, so that they also might be sanctified by the truth." Jesus has previously spoken of dying "for" his disciples (for example, 6:51, 10:15). His sanctification here appears to be sanctification for his sacrificial death. The only similar sanctification of a sacrifice in the Old Testament is the sanctification of the firstborn animals for sacrifice (Exodus 13:2, Deuteronomy 15:19-23). Remember that their sanctification recalls God's sanctification of the firstborn through the original Passover sacrifice. Jesus is alluding to the Passover and to its relationship to his death. He sanctifies himself, like the firstborn animal, to be the true Passover sacrifice that both recalls and fulfills the Passover.

Jesus sanctifies himself so that his disciples might be sanctified in the truth. The thought here is very similar to John 8:31-32 where true disciples remain in Jesus' word, come to know the truth, and are set free by it. His disciples are sanctified by remaining in the truth, because all those who remain in the truth will be sanctified by the Spirit. Jesus prays for this, because it has not happened yet. It depends upon his death and the gift of the Spirit. When the Spirit sanctifies the disciples of Jesus, he does so through the sanctifying blood of Jesus (1 Peter 1:2). Their sanctification is one of the benefits of his sacrificial death and further connects his sacrificial death to the fulfillment of the Passover and the blood of the covenant.

As we saw in the section on the Passover, sanctification logically belongs with making atonement and cleansing from sin. Similarly, becoming a child of God through eating Jesus' flesh and drinking his blood also implies that Jesus' sacrificial death makes atonement. How could one become a child of God apart from reconciliation to him through making atonement? In this section, we have seen how eating Jesus' flesh and drinking his blood through the Spirit fulfills the original Passover, including the application of the blood and the Passover meal. In the next section, we will see John's presentation of Jesus as the Lamb of God who takes away the sin of the world. This is where the atoning significance of Jesus' death comes to the forefront.

We have just gone over a few great truths that many Christians do not understand very well. If you ask Christians when they ate Jesus' flesh and drank his blood, most will be puzzled or point to the Lord's Supper. Of course, the Lord's Supper does have something to do with partaking of the body and blood of Jesus, but the Lord's Supper does not save people and give eternal life. At the Lord's Supper, we celebrate Jesus' sacrificial death for us. As we reflect on John 6:51-58, we see that the Lord's Supper also celebrates and recalls the moment when the Spirit fed us with the flesh and blood of Jesus. When we received these from the Spirit, we became children of God, saved by the sacrifice of the Lamb of God. We are thankful for the life-giving flesh and blood of the Lamb. May we celebrate these gifts with fervor and adoration.

The Lamb of God Who Delivers the Children of God from Sin and Death

God frees believers from sin and the devil by making them his children. Since God frees his children by the sanctifying blood of the Lamb, their salvation from bondage depends upon Jesus' fulfillment of the Passover sacrifice. In the case of the Passover sacrifice, we saw that it is clearly tied to sanctification and that sanctification is not possible without making atonement and cleansing from sin. The sanctifying blood of the Lamb cannot sanctify believers for God without making atonement for them and cleansing them from sin. The Gospel of John emphasizes making atonement more than sanctifying or cleansing, because his primary concern is the second aspect of the Passover. He means to show that the Lamb of God's sacrifice delivers believers from death. The cause of death is sin and God's judgment on sin. Without deliverance from death, freedom from bondage to sin and the devil has little meaning. The living Father intends for his children to be alive as well (John 6:57). At Passover time, Jesus dies so that believers might have eternal life. He abundantly fulfills the Passover sacrifice. Eating his flesh and drinking his blood fully delivers believers from death so that they can enjoy eternal life as the children of God.

Up to this point, we have not looked at two of John's key verses regarding the fulfillment of the Passover. Many interpreters see John 1:29 and 19:36 as the two most obvious verses related to the fulfillment of the Passover. In John 1:29, John the Baptist sees Jesus and says, "Behold, the Lamb of God who takes away the sin of the world." Later, Jesus dies at Passover time. John explicitly connects the death of Jesus to the Passover lamb. He says, "For these things happened so that the Scripture might be fulfilled, 'His (or its) bone will not be broken'" (19:36). John is quoting from either Exodus 12:46 or Numbers 9:12, where God tells his people not to break any of the bones of the Passover sacrifice. John is pointing to a typological fulfillment here, because this law concerning the Passover sacrifice is not a direct prophecy.

Although the Passover sacrifice could be a lamb or a young goat, the combination of John 1:29 and 19:36 has persuaded many interpreters through the centuries that the

Gospel of John presents Jesus as fulfilling the Passover sacrifice. Recent interpreters have struggled with this assessment, because they do not see a significant connection between the Passover sacrifice and taking away sin. As we are about to see, the Gospel of John links sin to death. In light of this link, it is possible to make a strong case for the fulfillment of the Passover sacrifice. Compared to the Passover sacrifice, is any other Old Testament sacrifice more closely related to deliverance from death?

"Sin" is not a common term in the Gospel of John. After the introduction of Jesus as the "Lamb of God who takes away the sin of the world" (1:29), we do not learn about sin and the danger of sin until John 8:21-51. We have already seen that John 8:31-47 teaches about slavery to sin and the devil. In John 8:21-24, Jesus connects sin to death. Jesus tells his audience that he is going away and that they cannot come where he is going. He is returning to the Father who sent him (7:33). While he is "from above" and "not of this world," they are "from below" and "of this world" (8:23). The only way to the Father is through faith in Jesus (14:6). Believers become children of God who are "not of the world" (17:14). They will eventually be with Jesus where he is (14:3). In the meantime, the Father and the Son are already with them (14:23).

Jesus addresses the consequences of unbelief in John 8:21-24. He says, "Therefore, if you do not believe that I am, you will die in your sins" (8:24). Believing in Jesus as God ("I am") is necessary for deliverance from death and sin. To die "in your sins" probably means to die "because of your sins."[9] We can see this by looking at Ezekiel 18:18, 24, 26, where we find very similar language to John 8:24 in the Septuagint. In these verses, sinners die because of their sins. We can also see this by looking at other parallels in John.

We can see that death is because of sin, especially unbelief, if we look at John's teaching on judgment and wrath. While the believer is free from God's judgment, Jesus says that an unbeliever is judged already, "because he has not believed in the name of the one and only Son of God" (John 3:18). God judges unbelievers, because of their chief sin, which is unbelief. In a related statement, John tells us that the one who believes in Jesus has eternal life, and "the one who disobeys the Son will not see life, but the wrath of God remains on him" (3:36). John here presents unbelief as disobedience to the Son. The consequence for this disobedience is death, which results from experiencing the wrath of God against sin. John 5:29 anticipates a future judgment in which those who do evil deeds will be judged. Escape from judgment is possible now for those who believe in Jesus. Escaping judgment means that the believer "has passed out of death into life" (5:24). Belief is the chief act of obedience that frees a person from God's judgment on sin, which is death.

Why is unbelief such a serious sin? John 8:24 provides part of the answer when it says that people will die due to their sins, if they do not "believe that I am." Unbelief is the most serious sin, because believing in Jesus is the only way to be delivered from judgment and death due to one's sins. Belief in Jesus delivers from sin, because Jesus delivers believers from sin. Jesus is the "I am," which means that he is the Lord. The Father has given Jesus the authority to judge (5:22). The Father has also sent him to deliver believers from sin and judgment by dying for his sheep (10:11).

Jesus' death delivers believers from sin, judgment, wrath, and death by making atonement for their sins. He does so, because he is the "Lamb of God who takes away the sin of the world" (1:29). As a result of committing sin, people "have sin" or "are guilty of sin." John 15:22-24 shows this with respect to the sin of hating Jesus and his Father. They will die due to their sin unless they believe in Jesus (8:24). When people believe in Jesus, Jesus takes away their sin and guilt for sin. He dies at Passover time as the Lamb of God in order to take away their sins through his sacrificial death. As we saw above, he then sends the Spirit to bring the benefits of his sacrificial death to all who believe. Through the Spirit, believers eat his flesh and drink his blood. His sacrificial death delivers believers from sin and death. By doing so, his death makes it possible for them to have eternal life (6:47, 51-58).

We can see that his death is a sacrifice of atonement, because it takes away sin and reconciles believers to God. Recall John 6:56, which says, "The one who eats my flesh and drinks my blood remains in me and I in him." Remaining in Jesus means unity with him. Unity with Jesus is the result of reconciliation and means unity with the Father as well (17:21-23). Reconciliation to God through sacrifice for sin points to Jesus' sacrificial death as a sacrifice of atonement. In 1 John 2:2, John speaks about the death of Jesus as a "propitiation" or "sacrifice of atonement" for sins.

What does Jesus' deliverance of his people from sin, judgment, wrath, and death have to do with the fulfillment of the Passover? We will be able to see this if we look for a moment at the bigger picture. The people in the world are in slavery to sin and the devil, who is the ruler of the world and their father (John 8:44, 12:31, 14:30, 16:11). The world has a second liability. Service to sin and the devil stains the people in the world with sin and guilt, which alienates them from God. They will experience God's wrath and judgment on sin, which means death.

The Father sends Jesus into the world to free his people from slavery and deliver them from sin and death. Jesus does so by dying as the Lamb of God who takes away the sins of the world (1:29). The people of God distinguish them-selves from the people of the world by believing in Jesus. Believers receive the Spirit who feeds them with the flesh and blood of Jesus. Jesus' blood makes atonement for their sins to reconcile them to God. His blood also sanctifies them, which makes them children of God. They have God as their Father and serve him rather than the devil. The people of God experience the fulfillment of the Passover when they believe in Jesus.

The people of the world are already under God's judgment due to their sin, especially their unbelief, and will experience sin's penalty, death (3:18, 8:24). In the future, they will experience God's final judgment and death due to sin (5:29). Although we dare not venture into it very far at this point, the devil also experiences God's judgment due to the death of Jesus. His immediate judgment is to be "cast out" (12:31), which may refer to being cast down from heaven to earth (Revelation 12:7-12). He will eventually also experience the second death (Revelation 20:10, 14).

The Passover prefigures the picture presented above. As the type or shadow, it anticipates its antitype or fulfillment. A few key points will illustrate the correspondence between them. The Passover involves God's climactic plague on Pharaoh and Egypt. They experience his judgment and wrath, which brings death (Exodus 6:6, Psalm 78:49-51). In preparation for this plague, the Father instructs his people to sacrifice the Passover lamb. God's people sacrifice the Passover lamb, which is an act of obedience that shows at least some measure of faith on their part. The Passover lamb makes atonement for the firstborn sons, which delivers them from God's judgment or death. It also sanctifies them for God. By doing so, it transfers them to God's ownership. They belong to God and are rightly his servants. Therefore, God frees them from slavery to Pharaoh and the Egyptians so that they can serve him.

Of course, the type does not perfectly correspond to the fulfillment. For instance, the Passover lamb temporarily saves the firstborn sons from death, but Jesus, the Lamb of God, saves all of his people from death completely and fully. They have eternal life. The correspondences between type and fulfillment are impressive enough for us to see that the Passover prefigures its fulfillment in the death of Jesus. The Passover is a major instance in which Moses did write about Jesus, just as Jesus claims in John 5:46.

Reflection and Conclusion

Since we have just seen how John's Passover theme fits together, it seems fitting to draw out a few of the implications of the chapter rather than summarize it again. Regarding the Passover itself, we saw that God designed it as a time for remembrance and thanksgiving. The Passover sacrifice itself points to this, since it is more similar to a thanksgiving peace offering than to other sacrifices. Jesus means for the Lord's Supper to be a time of remembrance and thanksgiving as well. At the Lord's Supper, we are to remember our salvation from sin, death, and slavery. We have also designed Easter for this purpose. We should teach the meaning of the death of Jesus and celebrate it well on both of these occasions.

When we celebrate Jesus' sacrificial death, we have a lot of truth that we can draw on and a lot for which to be thankful. His death has delivered believers from sin, judgment, wrath, and death. It freed us from slavery to sin and the devil. Jesus is our Lord who came down to reveal to us the real source of our struggles with sin and to redeem us. Slavery to sin and the devil sounds offensive, but it points to the gravity of the human condition. Slavery to sin and the devil leads to actual sinning, which alienates sinners from a holy God and leads to death. The Father sent the Son to give himself as the true sacrifice of atonement. Reconciliation to God means salvation, eternal life, and freedom. Who would dare to pass on such a generous offer? We are Christ's ambassadors. Let us teach the truth well and send out the call often, "be reconciled to God" (2 Corinthians 5:20).

Chapter 5

Hebrews 9: Entering into the True Tabernacle through the Blood of Jesus

—〰—

Many Christians have come across teaching about typology in relation to the Old Testament sacrifices. Somewhere along the way, many are taught that the Old Testament sacrifices anticipate Christ's death on the cross in some way. Interestingly, when I have browsed the shelves in theological libraries, the titles of books do not generally point to sacrificial typology as the most fascinating area of typology for authors to focus on. The most likely title in the library's section of books on typology is going to have something to do with the Tabernacle. Of course, these books at least touch on the sacrifices as types, but they tend to spend much of their time showing the typological, or sometimes allegorical, meaning of each piece of the Tabernacle. I am not sure why so many authors have devoted themselves to this endeavor, but they do provide support for an important truth regarding the Tabernacle and the Temple. God established them to be powerful instructional vehicles. It can be fascinating to meditate on what God communicates through them.

God set up the Tabernacle and the Temple to immerse the worshiper's senses with theologically significant experiences, including sights, sounds, and varying degrees of physical contact. Some Psalms idealize the Tabernacle or the Temple in a way that further heightens its draw as the ideal place for the servant of God. Where else on earth would one rather be than worshiping in the Tabernacle or the Temple, especially during a festival like the Passover or Feast of Tabernacles? Surely, God's house is the most blessed, secure, and lovely place to dwell in all of the earth, because the almighty God dwells there.[1] One day in the courts of the Temple is better than a thousand elsewhere (Psalm 84:10). The righteous are like healthy palm trees planted in the house of God, which is a picture of a blessed, secure, and long life (Psalm 92:12-14). Indeed, one of the disciples of Jesus is so impressed with the Temple that he exclaims, "Teacher, behold how great are the stones and the buildings!" (Mark 13:1). Given these and other wonderful things said about the Tabernacle and the Temple in the Bible, it is no wonder that the Temple was such a treasured part of the life of God's people in the first century.

The author of the book of Hebrews lived in the first century and was well aware of the special place of the Temple in the affections of the Jews, or Hebrews, as they were also called (Philippians 3:5). It is likely that he is concerned with explaining the gospel to Jewish Christians in order to encourage them to remain faithful to Christ. In doing so, he provides us with a rich example of typology in relation to the Tabernacle, Temple, and sacrifices.

A central point of his typology has to do with access to God. As imperfect types, the Tabernacle, Temple, and sacrifices only allowed for limited access to the Holy of Holies, which represents God's special dwelling place in the midst of his people. They were quite effective, however, in prefiguring the realities that would open up the way into the True Holy Place of God in heaven. The author of Hebrews makes this point by focusing our attention first on the nature and setup of the Tabernacle/Temple. Then, he moves on to the role of the sacrifices in securing access into the Tabernacle's Holy of Holies. He is especially attentive to the Day of Atonement, because its sacrifices are uniquely associated with the High Priest's entry into the Holy of Holies.

By examining the course of his teaching through Hebrews 8-9, we can learn a lot about typology in general and the typology of Temple and sacrifice in particular. Of course, learning about typology is not our only goal. Hebrews 8-9 directs our attention to the benefits of Christ's sacrificial death for us. His death provides the unique sacrifice of atonement that cleanses believers from sin, so that they can draw near to God in his True Temple. Drawing near to God is the privilege of those who have been reconciled to God through the atoning sacrifice of his Son. If one day in the courts of the Jerusalem Temple is better than a thousand elsewhere (Psalm 84:10), how much more could we say about the goodness of drawing near to God in his True Temple, which is in heaven and will one day be on earth (Revelation 21-22)? Due to Jesus' sacrificial death, our sin no longer renders us unfit to draw near to God. In this chapter, we will examine the cleansing and sanctifying power of Jesus' blood.

The Tabernacle on Earth vs. the True Tabernacle in Heaven (Hebrews 8:1-6)

In Hebrews 8:1-6, the author of Hebrews begins his treatment of the Tabernacle. He says that Jesus is our High Priest in heaven, where he is a minister in the Holy Place, the True Tabernacle, which God set up (8:1-2).[2] As we saw in chapter one, "true" is an adjective used several times in the Gospel of John to describe antitypes to the Old Testament types. In Hebrews, it occurs twice in reference to the Tabernacle or Holy Place in heaven (8:2, 9:24). In John and Hebrews, the adjective "true" is being used in the sense of "real" or "genuine." Thus the True Tabernacle is the "real" or "genuine" tabernacle.

By comparison, the Tabernacle on earth is a "copy and shadow of the heavenly things," where priests on earth serve according to the Law of Moses (Hebrews 8:4-5). In support of this, Hebrews 8:5 recalls that God said to Moses, "See that you make everything according to the pattern (*typos*) which was shown to you on the mountain" (Exodus 25:40 in the Septuagint). One finds here some common terms used in typology, like "shadow" and "pattern." They are used differently, because they are describing the relationship between the true or real entity in heaven and its imperfect shadow on earth. The author of Hebrews appears to be saying that God showed Moses the True Tabernacle in heaven when he was on Mount Sinai. God commanded him to make the Tabernacle on earth in such a way that it would conform to the pattern, the True Tabernacle. In saying this, the author is revealing the superiority of the True Tabernacle. It is the greater, more ancient dwelling place of God. The Tabernacle on earth is a copy and shadow that will always pale in comparison to it.

As other interpreters have noticed, the author does create a somewhat confusing situation for us when he chooses to use terminology in this way. He calls the Tabernacle of Moses a copy and shadow of the true one in heaven (8:5, 9:24). He does this in a section where the Law of Moses is said to contain the shadow of the good things to come (10:1). We are about to see that the Tabernacle and its sacrifices are indeed a shadow of the good things to come. So, the Tabernacle of Moses is a shadow in two respects. It is an imperfect shadow of the True Tabernacle in heaven. As such, it also is a shadow that prefigures the good things to come that will open up access to the True Holy Place, as seen in Hebrews 9-10.

Even more confusing for us as readers is the implication that the True Tabernacle is being presented as both a type and antitype in Hebrews 8-10. An important distinction may clarify the root of the confusion and help us to sort it out. One part of the picture in Hebrews 8-10 is of the True Tabernacle in heaven versus the Tabernacle on earth. The True Tabernacle in heaven is presented as the "type" or "pattern" for the Tabernacle on earth (8:5). As we will see, this makes the Tabernacle on earth its "antitype" (9:24), because "antitype" means something like "corresponding to the type." At this point, we are not yet dealing with typology, because we have defined typology as having to do with a type that prefigures an antitype that comes later and fulfills it.

A second part of the picture is developed in Hebrews 9-10. The Tabernacle on earth and the sacrifices that occur there are set up to prefigure the events that will one day occur in the True Tabernacle in heaven. Now we are dealing with typology proper. It may help to summarize the situation this way. The Tabernacle on earth is a copy and shadow of the True Tabernacle in heaven. As a copy and shadow of the True Tabernacle, its setup reflects the setup of the True Tabernacle. Sacrifices that take place in the Tabernacle prefigure the sacrifice of Christ that will one day open up the way into the True Tabernacle. This is where typology comes in.

Now, before leaving Hebrews 8:1-6, we need to look at a few pieces of the bigger picture from the Old Testament to appreciate why the author of Hebrews has directed our attention to the Tabernacle and the True Tabernacle in heaven. First, why does he focus on the Tabernacle instead of the Temple? The Tabernacle was long gone by his time and the Temple built by Herod was a far more grand representation of heavenly things than the Tabernacle. The best answer focuses on the fact that the author is making a biblical case that ultimately involves the grand fulfillment of what the Tabernacle, Temple, and their sacrificial system represent.[3]

God revealed the Tabernacle and its sacrificial system to the greatest prophet of the Old Testament, Moses (Hebrews 8:5, Exodus 25:40). The focus on the sacrificial system in Hebrews 9-10 points back to Moses and the Tabernacle. It is true that God also later revealed the pattern for the Temple to David (1 Chronicles 28:19), but David does not make significant changes to the sacrificial system and the basic Temple setup is obviously patterned after the Tabernacle.

A look back at the Old Testament also helps us to appreciate why the author of Hebrews directs our attention to the True Tabernacle in heaven. The Old Testament is already quite aware of the limited sense in which the Tabernacle, and later the Temple, is God's dwelling place. God's throne in the Holy of Holies above the Ark of the Covenant is his throne on earth.[4] In truth, God is enthroned in heaven and the Tabernacle/Temple is merely his footstool.[5] Thus, the Old Testament shows that heaven, rather than earth, is God's true dwelling place.

Given these pieces of Old Testament background, the author of Hebrews is going to show us that the Old Testament precursors are pointing to something greater. If God's dwelling place in heaven provides the pattern for the Tabernacle on earth, then the Tabernacle's sacrifices should have heavenly counterparts as well. Just like the Tabernacle in heaven is far greater than the one on earth, these sacrifices would surely be greater than their counterparts on earth. But what kind of sacrifices are suitable for offering in heaven? What is the purpose of these sacrifices?

What the Holy Spirit Teaches Us about the Way into the Holy of Holies (Hebrews 9:1-10)

So far, we know that Jesus is the High Priest of the True Tabernacle in heaven who has a sacrifice to offer there (8:4). Now, in Hebrews 9, the author reveals that Jesus is also the sacrifice. Hebrews 9:1-10 focuses our attention on what the Holy Spirit teaches about the way into the Holy of Holies by means of the setup of the Tabernacle and its sacrificial system.

Hebrews 9:1-10 begins with a summary of the basic layout of the Tabernacle (vv. 1-5). One finds here the important aspects of the Tabernacle familiar from the Old Testament.[6] Hebrews 9:6-7 moves on to the rules for entering into the Holy Place and the Holy of Holies. The priests are "continually," or "regularly," going into and out of the "first tabernacle," that is, the Holy Place (9:2, 6). Access to the "second tabernacle," the Holy of Holies, is much more restricted (9:3, 7). Only the High Priest can go in there and only once a year, on the Day of Atonement (Leviticus 16). He enters with blood from sin offerings for his sins and the sins of the people (Hebrews 9:7, Leviticus 16:11-15).

According to Hebrews 9:8, the Holy Spirit is teaching something through the limited access of the High Priest into the second tabernacle, the Holy of Holies. He is teaching that God has not yet revealed the way into the Holy of Holies while the first tabernacle still occupies its status as the Holy Place.[7] This teaching is important enough to deserve some clarification. The Holy Spirit revealed the setup for the Tabernacle to Moses, as well as rules for entry into the Holy Place and the Holy of Holies. By severely restricting access to the Holy of Holies, the Holy Spirit is teaching God's people that God has not yet revealed the way for his people to approach his throne in the Holy of Holies. These limitations of access continue in force as long as the Law of Moses continues in force to support the need for two tabernacles, an inner one and an outer one. Ultimately, there will be no need for an outer tabernacle, the Holy Place, because the way into the Holy of Holies will be open and God's priests will be able to perform their duties there. This is what the author means at the end of 9:8, when he says, "while the first (or outer) tabernacle still has its place."

It was probably clearer in the ancient world that the Holy Spirit was indicating something special by the limitations on access into the Holy of Holies. For instance, a relevant story is found in the first chapter of 3 Maccabees, a Jewish work written around the time of Jesus. Ptolemy IV, the king of Egypt, comes to Jerusalem to worship. He decides that he wants to enter the Holy of Holies. Ptolemy is surprised when he is greeted with great resistance. The Jews explain to him the Law of Moses concerning the High Priest's limited access into the Holy of Holies (1:11). He explains to them that he has never encountered resistance when he has visited other temples and entered them (1:13). Clearly, Ptolemy thought it was strange to have such strict rules about entry into a temple. He brought up a question that others, including Jews, must have asked from time to time, namely, "why are we not allowed to go in there?"

The author of Hebrews provides the reason for the limited access in the next two verses. The outer tabernacle, the Holy Place, is a "figure" or "symbol" (*parabolē*) with significance for the present time (9:9a). In the case of the "figure," "gifts and sacrifices are offered which cannot make the worshiper perfect with respect to conscience, because they are only regulations for the flesh concerned with food and drink and various washings" (9:9-10).[8] He goes on to say that they are only in force "until the time of reformation" (9:10). Thus, the "figure" is the outer tabernacle and the sacrifices associated with it. It is about to become clear that this "figure" is equivalent to a type (10:1).[9] It is an imperfect shadow that prefigures the antitypes to come in the "time of reformation." The central contrast set up here is between an internal effect and a merely external one. The sacrifices have an effect upon the flesh (external), but not upon perfecting the worshiper's conscience (internal).

It is now possible to sum up the main point of Hebrews 9:1-10. The sacrifices were not adequate to perfect anyone so that they could enter regularly into the Holy of Holies. In comparison, priests regularly enter into the Holy Place to serve God there. When the High Priest does enter the Holy of Holies once a year, he must enter with the blood of a sacrifice for his sins or he will die (Leviticus 16:2). Even he is not holy enough to enter into the presence of God in the Holy of Holies. The Tabernacle and its sacrificial system are inadequate to prepare anyone to enter into the presence of God in his Tabernacle on earth. How much more inadequate must they be for preparing anyone to enter into the presence of God in his True Tabernacle in heaven? The author of Hebrews has done a good job of highlighting the inadequacy of the Old Testament types, but we are about to see how important these types are for anticipating the solution to the imperfection of the worshiper.

The Blood of Christ Fulfills the Day of Atonement by Cleansing Believers from Sin and Death (Hebrews 9:11-14)

Hebrews 9:11-14 provides the initial outworking of the sacrificial typology that was anticipated in the previous verses. In these verses, the author moves back and forth between the Old Testament types and their fulfillments in Christ. Leviticus 16 is the most important Old Testament source to which he alludes in these verses, because it is the most important chapter of the Old Testament in relation to the sacrifices and rituals of the Day of Atonement. The author shows us in these verses how wonderfully Christ fulfills the Day of Atonement. This fulfillment means fuller, deeper cleansing for the people of God. It reaches within them to cleanse their consciences from "dead works" so that they might serve the "living God" (9:14).

In Hebrews 9:11-12, the description of the events of the True Day of Atonement begins. Christ is the main actor. He is the High Priest "of the good things to come," the one who ushers in the good things that the Day of Atonement prefigured (9:11). The scene for the True Day of Atonement is the "greater and more perfect" Tabernacle to which the Tabernacle on earth pales in comparison. Christ enters the True Holy Place "once for all," "through his own blood" (9:12). By comparison, the High Priest entered the Holy of Holies "once a year" (9:7) with the "blood of goats and calves" (9:12). He offers the blood of the calf for his own sins and impurities, while the goat is for the sins and impurities of the people (9:7, Leviticus 16:3-14). Christ only brings the blood from one sacrifice, which is for the sins of the people, because he is not a sinner who needs to offer a sacrifice for his own sins as well (7:26-28).

The next focus of the author of Hebrews is to compare the cleansing power of certain Old Testament sacrifices to that of the blood of Christ. He refers to both the "blood of goats and bulls" and to the "ashes of a heifer" (9:13). What do the blood and the ashes of the heifer accomplish? The author says that they "sanctify them for the cleansing (or purification) of their flesh" (9:13). The basis for this claim is found in the Old Testament. On the Day of Atonement (Leviticus 16), the blood of a bull and a goat is offered. One of their purposes is to make atonement for all of the priests and the people (Leviticus 16:33). The context clarifies that "making atonement" is an action that is closely related to both cleansing and sanctifying.[10] For instance, Leviticus 16:30 says that atonement is made for the people in order to cleanse them from their sins. In the case of sanctification, Leviticus 16:18 talks about making atonement for the altar. Leviticus 16:19 goes over the same ground again, but talks about cleansing it and sanctifying it. In Leviticus 16, the main emphasis is upon cleansing and becoming clean through the Day of Atonement sacrifices. These sacrifices of atonement cleanse the people and the priests from all of their sins (16:30, 33). They also cleanse the Tabernacle, the Holy of Holies, and the altar from Israel's sins and impurities (16:16-19, 33).

What about the ashes of a heifer? The ashes of a heifer do not occur anywhere in the Day of Atonement rituals. Without warning, the author of Hebrews includes a reference to another Old Testament type (Numbers 19). Like the bull and goat for the Day of Atonement, the ashes of the red heifer is a purification offering (Numbers 19:9). It usually has a very specific purpose, namely, to purify someone who has become unclean due to direct or indirect contact with a dead person (19:12). According to the Law of Moses, contact with a dead person causes one of the most serious forms of ritual impurity or uncleanness. In fact, a basic point underlying various ritual purity regulations is to separate God's people from death and to cleanse them from impurity arising from contact with death.[11] Anyone who comes into contact with a dead person must be cleansed from impurity with the ashes of the heifer. One who is not cleansed from impurity in this way is defiling the Tabernacle where God dwells and must be cut off from God's people (Numbers 19:12, 20).[12]

The author of Hebrews has chosen a type, the ashes of a heifer, that is quite relevant for his purposes, because he is anticipating part of his statement about the efficacy of the blood of Christ. Notice that the blood of the heifer is one component of the ashes (Numbers 19:5). In Hebrews 9:14, he says that the blood of Jesus cleanses the conscience from "dead works to serve the living God." So, the ashes of the heifer is a type in that it cleanses the flesh from impurity caused by contact with a dead person. As its antitype, the blood of Jesus provides internal cleansing of the conscience from the impurity caused by "dead works."[13] "Dead works" are sinful works that belong to the order of death, because they ultimately bring death to the sinner.[14] Impurity from death hinders the worshiper from approaching "the living God" (9:14).

Table 5: Summary of Hebrews 9 Types and Antitypes			
Type and Old Testament Texts	Benefit(s) of Type	Antitype in Hebrews 9	Benefit(s) of Antitype
Sacrifices of atonement, especially on Day of Atonement (Lev. 16)	Cleanses flesh from sin (Heb. 9:13)	Sacrificial death of Christ	Cleanses conscience or the heart from an evil conscience (Heb. 9:14, 10:22)
Ashes of heifer, which includes blood (Num. 19)	Cleanses flesh of impurity from contact with death (Heb. 9:13)	Blood of Christ	Cleanses conscience from dead works (Heb. 9:14)
a) Moses cleanses Tabernacle with blood when it is set up (Lev. 8) b) High priest cleanses Tabernacle every year on Day of Atonement (Lev. 16)	Cleanses and sanctifies Tabernacle to make it a fit dwelling place for God where priests and people have limited access to his throne on earth (Heb. 9:21-23)	One-time sacrifice of Christ cleanses the True Holy Place in heaven by fully cleansing the people of God from sin	Opens up free access to God's true throne in heaven for all of God's people who are able to approach him and offer spiritual sacrifices (Heb. 9:23-24, 10:19-22)

When one brings the Day of Atonement sacrifices together with the ashes of the heifer, the focus of Hebrews 9:10-14 becomes clearer. As the antitype to Day of Atonement sacrifices, the blood of Jesus fully cleanses people from the uncleanness caused by their sins. It cleanses the conscience (internal cleansing), rather than merely cleansing the flesh (external cleansing). Because sins are "dead works," they defile the conscience with uncleanness or impurity arising from constant contact with death. The conscience must be fully cleansed from sin and death if the worshiper is going to be "perfect in conscience" (9:9). A perfect conscience is a must in order to enter God's True Holy Place and "serve the living God" as his priests (9:14). As one learns from the Tabernacle on earth, unclean entry into the Holy of Holies will result in the penalty of death (Leviticus 16:2). Also, failure to be cleansed from death defiles the Tabernacle, so it is a sin worthy of death or expulsion from the people of God (Numbers 19:12, 20).

The focus on cleansing from sin and death in Hebrews 9:13-14 may provide a significant clue to help us understand the description of Christ as one "who through an eternal spirit offered himself *amōmos* (without blemish or without sin) to God" (9:14). Christ himself was *amōmos*. This term can refer to a sacrificial animal's freedom from physical defects ("without blemish"), but it is usually used in the New Testament with reference to a person's freedom from sin ("blameless" or "without sin"). The second meaning is probably primary here. Christ was fully clean from sin, so he was both a worthy sacrifice to be offered to God and a worthy priest to enter into the True Holy Place in heaven.[15]

How Does Christ's Blood Cleanse the True Holy Place?
(Hebrews 9:21-28)

The concern up to this point has been with cleansing the worshiper. In the next section, the cleansing of the True Tabernacle itself moves to the forefront. The very idea of the cleansing of the True Tabernacle raises a host of questions for interpreters. For instance, when or how was it ever polluted by sin or uncleanness? If it has never been polluted, how does one account for its cleansing? The best approach to these questions is to examine Hebrews 9:21-28 as part of the author's typological argument in Hebrews 9.

Hebrews 9:15-20 are a brief, but necessary departure from the fulfillment of the Day of Atonement. These verses deal with covenant typology, but its implications are not fully developed at this point. Here it focuses on the correspondence between the old and new covenants in relationship to inauguration through death and blood. The most significant element of these verses for our purposes is Moses' sprinkling of all of the people with the blood of calves and goats, which is the "blood of the covenant" (9:19-20). The author waits until 10:29 to indicate explicitly that he views the blood of the old covenant as a type for the blood of the new covenant, which sanctifies believers.

In Hebrews 9:21, the author makes the curious claim that Moses also sprinkled the Tabernacle and all of its vessels with the blood. The claim is curious, because one cannot find straightforward Old Testament evidence that Moses himself did this. The author of Hebrews may have been drawing out the implications that he saw in several other verses. Alternatively, he may have been agreeing with or following other Jewish interpreters who were drawing out the implications of several other verses. For instance, Josephus says much the same thing. He claims that Moses consecrated the Tabernacle and its vessels with both oil and blood.[16] According to the Old Testament, Moses sprinkled the Tabernacle, the altar, and its vessels (or utensils) with oil to consecrate them (Leviticus 8:10-11, Exodus 40:9-11). Later, he purified the altar with blood (8:15). Similarly, he anoints Aaron with oil (8:12). Then, Moses anoints Aaron again. This time he does so with both oil and blood (8:30). By implication, one might assume that anointing with oil precedes sprinkling with blood in the case of the rest of the Tabernacle and its vessels. Also, on the Day of Atonement, the High Priest sprinkles blood in the Holy of Holies and on the main altar (Leviticus 16:14-15, 19). It is possible that he sprinkles blood elsewhere in the Tabernacle as well, because the summary statements mention making atonement for the Tabernacle, Holy of Holies and the altar (Leviticus 16:16, 20, 33).[17] If the Tabernacle needs to be cleansed with blood every year, then one might assume that it was cleansed with blood at its inception as well. Moses' one-time cleansing of the Tabernacle with blood is going to be important below, because it is an important type for Jesus' cleansing of the True Tabernacle.

The next two statements are less surprising. They provide two general principles of sacrificial typology that anticipate the contents of Hebrews 9:23-28. The first principle states, "Almost all things are cleansed with blood, according to the Law" (Hebrews 9:22a). One can find abundant evidence for this in Leviticus. Leviticus 16 provides a convenient example, because it is directly concerned with the Day of Atonement. On the Day of Atonement, the priests, the people, and the Tabernacle are cleansed with blood (16:33). According to the second principle, "without shedding of blood forgiveness does not take place" (Hebrews 9:22b). This principle is also assumed to be from the Law of Moses. One can find illustrations for it in several verses of Leviticus 4-5, where making atonement through the offering of a sacrifice is closely associated with forgiveness of sin.

The first general principle of Hebrews 9:22 complements 9:21 in relation to the sprinkling of the Tabernacle with blood. By means of the first general principle, the author clarifies that the Law requires the Tabernacle and its vessels to be sprinkled with blood in order to cleanse them. In 9:23, the author begins to draw out the implications of 9:21-22 for the True Tabernacle in heaven. The logic depends upon a typological relationship. The Law contains the type, namely, Moses' cleansing of the Tabernacle with blood. This type is prefiguring its antitype, Christ's cleansing of the True Tabernacle with blood. Therefore, the necessity for cleansing the Tabernacle on earth points in advance to the necessity for cleansing the Tabernacle in heaven. As one moves from type to antitype, one must take into account the fact that the True Tabernacle is superior to the Tabernacle on earth, because the one on earth is a mere copy of the True Tabernacle (9:23, 8:1-5). As a result, one arrives at the claim made in 9:23 that the True Tabernacle and its vessels must be cleansed with "better sacrifices" (9:23).

The author does not pause to clarify why it would ever be necessary to cleanse the True Tabernacle. Interpreters have often tried to figure out the answer to this mystery.[18] The best answers are those that recognize the absurdity of trying to envision some reason for the True Tabernacle to be unclean in some way. The author already asserted in Hebrews 9:8-9 that the way into the Holy Place on earth was not open prior to the sacrifice of Christ. Old Testament sacrifices were not able to perfect the conscience of the worshiper. Therefore, the Holy of Holies was not accessible, because a worshiper stained with sin and impurity could not safely enter into it. If this was true in the case of the Tabernacle on earth, the greater Tabernacle in heaven was even more inaccessible and therefore secure against the entry of sinful, impure worshipers who would defile it.

When the author of Hebrews speaks about cleansing the True Tabernacle in heaven, he is directing our minds to the sacrifice of Christ. This sacrifice opens up the way in to the True Tabernacle in heaven, which was formerly closed to us due to our sin, guilt, and impurity (Hebrews 10:19-20). He appears to be combining two related types concerning the cleansing of the Tabernacle. In the case of the first type, Moses sprinkled the Tabernacle with blood once, at the initial establishment of the Tabernacle (9:21). The blood purifies it and sanctifies it from the sins and impurities of the people. This prepares the Tabernacle to be the place where God dwells in the midst of his people and where the priests and the people come to offer sacrifices and approach his throne on earth. The antitype to this is Christ's one-time cleansing of the True Tabernacle with blood in preparation for his priestly people to enter there and approach his throne in heaven.[19] According to the second type, the High Priest takes over the job of cleansing the Tabernacle from Moses. He cleanses the Tabernacle once a year with the blood of a bull and a goat in order to cleanse and sanctify it from the sins and impurities of the priests and the people. Then, Christ comes as the True High Priest who fulfills the Day of Atonement by cleansing the True Tabernacle once and for all with his own blood (Hebrews 9:24-28).

The dilemma created by both of these types is that the True Tabernacle does not need purification or sanctification. It is already what the Tabernacle ideally should be, that is, perfectly pure and holy. The two typologies both point to the source of the Tabernacle's need for cleansing. It needs cleansing due to contact with the sin and impurity of the people. If the people were perfectly pure and holy, then they would not defile the Tabernacle. Therefore, according to the antitype, Jesus only indirectly cleanses the True Tabernacle by directly cleansing his people with his blood before they draw near to God in the True Tabernacle (9:26, 10:19-22). This cleansing means that God's people will never pollute the True Tabernacle with their sin or impurity.[20] In other words, the blood of Jesus secures the perfection of those who are sanctified by it (10:14), which makes it possible for them to draw near to God without making the True Tabernacle unclean or unholy.[21]

In Hebrews 9:24, the author begins his treatment of Christ's cleansing by supporting his earlier claim (9:23) that the heavenly realities must be cleansed with better sacrifices than the sacrifices for cleansing the Tabernacle on earth. He points first to the superior nature of the Holy Place that Christ cleanses. As a superior Holy Place, it must be cleansed with a superior sacrifice. He establishes the Holy Place's superiority by making two points. First, Christ did not enter with his blood into "a holy place made with hands," like the Holy Place of the Tabernacle. God himself set up the Tabernacle in heaven (8:2). Second, the Tabernacle's Holy Place is only an "antitype" (*antitypa*) or "copy" of the "true" Holy Place. As we saw in the first section of this chapter, God showed the Tabernacle in heaven to Moses and commanded him to use it as the "type" or "pattern" for the Tabernacle on earth. The Tabernacle on earth is an earthly representation of a superior reality in heaven, the True Tabernacle (8:1-5).

When Christ entered into heaven, the True Tabernacle, he was truly entering into "the presence of God for us" (9:24). As noted earlier, the Old Testament presents the Tabernacle as the place of God's throne on earth, but God's true throne is in heaven.[22] As the True High Priest, Christ entered into God's very presence. Even Moses did not attain to such a privilege, even though he often met with God in the Tent of Meeting (Exodus 33:7-11).

If the heavenly Tabernacle is clearly a better and more perfect Tabernacle (9:24), in what respect is Christ a better and more perfect sacrifice? He is the one-time fulfillment of the Day of Atonement sacrifices. The High Priest enters the Holy of Holies on earth every year with the blood of bulls and goats. In contrast, Christ did not sacrifice himself "many times" or "again and again" (9:25). He did not suffer and die every year ever since the foundation of the world when the True Tabernacle was set up (9:26). On this point, his sacrifice is the antitype that is different from and superior to the sacrifices that preceded him. Christ "appeared once at the consummation of the ages for the removal of sin through sacrificing himself" (9:26). In other words, he came on the scene at the time of fulfillment to do what the previous sacrifices were incapable of doing. He came to remove sin definitively through offering one perfect sacrifice for sins. In doing so, he secures the cleansing of his people from sin so that they can draw near to God in the True Tabernacle without fear.

Hebrews 9:27-28 draws out another hopeful and inspiring implication of Christ's one-time, definitive sacrifice. Since Christ's sacrifice is a one-time event, he will next appear to his people to grant them the salvation that is the proper reward for the righteous. For our purposes, these verses are especially significant in that they contain an allusion to Isaiah 53:12. The author of Hebrews uses the same words here as the Septuagint when he says that Christ "bore the sins of many." Thus, Christ is the fulfillment of Isaiah's prophecy concerning the Suffering Servant. Isaiah 53 is an important prophecy, because it is so unique. The Suffering Servant provides an instance where a person and not a sacrificial animal is called a "guilt offering" (53:10, see Leviticus 5). Thus, it anticipates a sacrifice for sin, where the sacrifice is a person rather than an animal. Isaiah 53 is therefore an important contributor to sacrificial typology, because it points more directly to the form that the ultimate fulfillment of the sacrifices will take. In line with Isaiah 53, the author later supports the need for a greater sacrifice that involves human obedience rather than the sacrifice of an animal (Hebrews 10:5-9). Isaiah 53 provides an important illustration of the way in which a direct prophecy can point the way to the fulfillment of a type.

Conclusion

By the close of Hebrews 9, we have seen direct or indirect references to several Old Testament types. The Day of Atonement is conspicuous among the Old Testament types, but we have also noted the presence of other types, like the ashes of the heifer. It becomes clear that the author believes that God specifically designed the Tabernacle and its sacrifices to prefigure the better realities to come. The Tabernacle and its sacrifices teach something about what needs to happen in the True Tabernacle so that God's people can enter there. One sees indications that it is God's intention for his people to enter the True Tabernacle, because he has permitted his people to approach him in his Tabernacle on earth. The sin and impurity that limit their ability to approach him in his earthly Tabernacle also make it impossible for them to enter his Tabernacle in heaven.

In the fullness of time, Christ sacrifices himself to open up the way into the True Tabernacle by cleansing and perfecting the conscience of God's servants. Christ's blood provides the internal cleansing that cleanses the conscience from sin and death. As our High Priest, he brings his blood into God's True Temple so that we, too, might draw near to God and serve God as his priests. We have access to God that surpasses even the access of the High Priests under the old covenant. In the next chapter, we will see how the author of

Hebrews draws out the implications of our access to God in Hebrews 10:19-25.

Chapter 6

Hebrews 10: The Unique Sacrifice of the Messiah Takes away Sin

—✦—

In Hebrews 10:1-22, the author brings us to the conclusion and culmination of the Day of Atonement typology that he was developing in Hebrews 9. In his conclusion, he encourages us to appreciate and utilize the privilege of entry into the True Tabernacle (10:19-22). He builds toward his conclusion in three stages. The first stage brings out the purpose and imperfection of the Day of Atonement sacrifices (10:1-4). The second stage shows us where the Old Testament predicts that the obedience of the Messiah would bring the solution to the problem of sin that the sacrifices could never provide (10:5-10). David typology lies at the heart of this stage. The third stage amplifies the significance of Christ as the one who brings the fulfillment of the messianic expectations (10:11-18).

When you look at the description of these three stages and at Hebrews 10:1-18, what is the new and striking element that the author introduces here? It is in stage two, where we learn something new from David's words regarding sacrifice. As the type for Christ, David predicts the sacrifice of Christ when he speaks about doing God's will in place of offering animal sacrifices. Christ did God's will in offering himself on the cross. In doing so, he brings about the fulfillment of David's prediction and of the Old Testament sacrifices. As we already saw in Hebrews 9, Christ is the intersection point for multiple typological relationships. Hebrews 10:5-10 provides an interesting instance where David typology points the way to the antitype of the sacrifices, namely, the sacrifice of Christ. In order to appreciate the need for the sacrifice of Christ, Hebrews 10:1-4 begins this section by calling our attention to the prophetic purpose and the limitations of the Old Testament sacrifices.

What the Yearly Day of Atonement Sacrifices Teach about Sin (Hebrews 10:1-4)

Although Hebrews 10:1 repeats some points about the inadequacy of Old Testament sacrifices that are familiar to us from Hebrews 9, the author returns to these points, because he wants to spell out the message of these sacrifices. His focus up to this point has been on the shortcomings of the Old Testament sacrifices, especially those offered on the Day of Atonement. They do not perfect or cleanse the worshiper's conscience. So, they do not prepare the worshiper to enter into the Holy of Holies. What then is the purpose of these sacrifices? First, he states more clearly than he has done previously that they are imperfect prefigurations of the "good things to come" (10:1). Second, he makes the new point that the Day of Atonement sacrifices provide a yearly reminder of the sins of God's people (10:2-4). These sacrifices are reminders of the persistence of sin and the need for a solution to the problem of sin.

Hebrews 10:1 is an important verse for students of typology, because it provides a general statement about the Law of Moses. It says, "Since the Law has a shadow of the good things to come, not the form itself of the things, it is never able to perfect, by means of the same sacrifices that they offer endlessly year after year, the ones who are drawing near." Notice that the first part of the sentence tells the reader why the Law is never able to perfect the ones who are drawing near. It contains only a shadow, but the shadow is predictive of good things to come. It is not hard to see why Old Testament types become associated with a shadow, or shadows, due to this verse. Before and after, the context presents Old Testament sacrifices as imperfect prefigurations of the sacrifice of Christ. Earlier, in Hebrews 9:8-10, he told us that the Tabernacle and its sacrifices are a "figure" that has something to do with the present, the time of fulfillment. Now, he states more clearly that its sacrifices have to do with the present, because they contribute to the Law's shadow of things to come. The term "shadow" fits quite well with the idea of prediction while also suggesting impermanence in contrast to the realities themselves.

In case 10:1 did not go far enough in making his point about the imperfection of the Law's sacrifices, he draws out one of the implications of his point. Picking up on the endless yearly repetition of the sacrifices, he asks, "would they not have ceased being offered"? If they could perfect the worshipers, then the worshipers would have been cleansed once and afterwards have had no further "consciousness of sins" (10:2).[1] In other words, a sacrifice that could make one perfect would not need to be performed every year like the Day of Atonement sacrifices. It would cleanse the conscience once and deliver one from any "consciousness of sins."

The repetition of the sacrifices on the Day of Atonement reveals that they were not intended by God to perfect the worshiper. Instead, God intended them as "a yearly reminder of sins" (10:3). In other words, the Day of Atonement sacrifices reinforce a regular, yearly "consciousness of sins" rather than relieve it. The yearly reminder of sins is serious, because God is the one who set up the Day of Atonement to remind his people about their sins. God wants his people to remember their sins, because he remembers them as well.[2] Hebrews 10:3 therefore anticipates Hebrews 10:17-18, where God no longer remembers his people's sins. As we will see, the Day of Atonement's sacrifices are no longer necessary at that point due to the complete forgiveness of sins that is only possible because of the blood of Jesus.

When our author says, "it is impossible for the blood of bulls and goats to take away sins" (10:4), he is rephrasing his assessment of the Law's sacrifices (10:1). The proof for this point is found in 10:1-2. The Law's sacrifices are part of the shadow that points to the good things to come. Their repetition shows that they are not able to perfect the worshipers so that they are free from sin. In 10:4, the author reiterates his assessment of the sacrifices in preparation for the next section in which he is going to reveal the perfect sacrifice that does take away sins and renders the Day of Atonement sacrifices obsolete (10:5-18). In contrast to the imperfect types that preceded it, the perfect sacrifice will only be offered once and will relieve the worshiper's "consciousness of sins" (10:2).

David Predicts that the Christ Will Fulfill the Old Testament Sacrifices (Hebrews 10:5-10)

In order to make his next point, the author of Hebrews attributes the words of a Psalm of David directly to Christ and shows how these words fit perfectly with what Christ does to fulfill the Old Testament sacrifices (10:5-10). Most interpreters neglect to dwell upon reasons why it would be appropriate to apply these words to Christ and his work. In light of the rest of the New Testament, an assumed typological relationship between David and Christ is probably the best way to account for this quotation from Psalm 40:6-8.[3]

Recognizing the undergirding David typology is important, because it clarifies an important point about the quotation. The author of Hebrews regards these words from Psalm 40:6-8 as specifically applicable to the Christ, because he is the antitype to David. The Christ offered himself in order to accomplish the complete sanctification of God's people that the Old Testament sacrifices prefigured. As a result, Psalm 40:6-8 shines forth as a typological prophecy that anticipates the death of the Christ as the fulfillment of the Old Testament sacrifices. A closer look at Hebrews 10:5-10 will support these points and provide a closer examination of an important instance of David typology.

The most difficult aspect of Hebrews 10:5-10 comes first. The author introduces the quotation from Psalm 40 by saying, "Therefore, when he comes into the world, he says" (10:5). In light of Hebrews 9:11, 14, 24, 28, the "he" here is "Christ." "When he comes into the world" is a reference to the incarnation. It tells us that Christ says these words during his time in the world. [4] The difficult word is "says." Did Christ ever say these words? We have no record of them in the Gospels. The author of Hebrews does the same thing in 2:12-13, where he puts the words of David and Isaiah into the mouth of Jesus. In these cases, the author of Hebrews appears to be doing something that is unusual and he does not provide an explanation for us. It seems likely that he has noticed a significant commonality between the words of Jesus and the words of David in Psalm 40:6-8. In the Gospels, Jesus may not have ever quoted Psalm 40:6-8, but he comes close to its contents and the interpretation of its contents in Hebrews 10:8-10. We will return to the commonalities with the words of Jesus after we look at the contents and significance of the quotation.

The quotation from Psalm 40:6-8 in Hebrews 10:5-7 basically follows the Septuagint. It is important to notice the psalm's superscription. It is a psalm of David. The verses are set up in four parallel parts. The first ("sacrifice and offering you did not desire") and the third parts ("in burnt offerings and sacrifices for sin you did not delight") are mainly repetitive (Hebrews 10:5, 6). It is clearer in Hebrew than in Greek that the various terms for sacrifices used here refer to a variety of sacrifices required under the Law of Moses.[5] Therefore, David recognizes that the Old Testament sacrifices are not what God really wanted.

The second and fourth parts put forward what God does want (Hebrews 10:5b, 7). The structure of the verses suggests that these two parts are likely to be related just like the other two parts are related. "But a body you prepared for me" points to the body as the instrument of obedience (10:5b). The body is going to be the instrument used "to do your will" (10:7b). This fits very well in Hebrews, because he is about to establish a connection between doing God's will and Jesus' offering of his body. At first glance, it does not appear to fit with the Hebrew Old Testament, which has no mention of a body here. For some interpreters, this is a case where the author of Hebrews depends on the Septuagint and neglects the meaning of the Hebrew text. In Hebrew, Psalm 40:6 contains a difficult phrase often translated something like "my ears you have opened." The Septuagint translator has interpreted the opening of the ears to mean that God has prepared David's body for doing God's will. His interpretation rests upon the plausible assumption that the opening of the ears (40:6) prepares David for hearing God and doing his will (40:8). In other words, he is trying to stress that opening the ears prepares David's body for obedience, which is the focus of Psalm 40:8. As a result, the Septuagint translator has chosen to paraphrase the Hebrew text in a way that is consistent with its meaning.[6]

Why has the author of Hebrews chosen to follow the paraphrase contained in the Septuagint? Of course, it is possible that he is simply following the Septuagint without consideration for the Hebrew Old Testament.[7] However, even if he was aware of the Hebrew text, he might have chosen to follow the Septuagint translation, because it fits so well with the point he is making. God prepared a body for Christ as an instrument for doing God's will. Christ is going to do God's will by offering his body as the perfect sacrifice. The focus is on Christ's body, not his ears. This becomes clear in the verses after the quotation.

The author proceeds to interpret the quotation with reference to the fulfillment of the Old Testament sacrifices. In 10:8, he repeats all four words for sacrifices and offerings from the preceding quotation. He also repeats both verbs pertaining to them in order to show that God did not desire or delight in these sacrifices and offerings. He concludes with the reminder that they all "are offered according to the Law" (10:8). In 10:9, he repeats, "Behold, I have come to do your will," which also reminds us of the mention of Christ's coming in 10:5. Then, he draws his conclusion, "He takes away the first so that he might establish the second" (10:9). Here he emphasizes that Christ's obedience to God's will now replaces the sacrifices that prefigured and anticipated his sacrifice.[8] Hebrews 10:1 anticipates this point. Christ sets aside the Law's imperfect "shadow of the good things to come," when he establishes the true realities in their place. The Law's sacrifices belong to the temporary shadow. They predict the perfect sacrifice that will one day come to fulfill them as a permanent part of the new order.

Hebrews 10:10 spells out what Christ established in the place of the Old Testament sacrifices. The author of Hebrews is not merely saying that the sacrifices are replaced by Christ's obedience. He has a specific aspect of Christ's obedience in mind. It is true that Christ did God's will all of his life on earth, but the culmination of God's will for him involved offering himself as the perfect sacrifice.[9] So, he says, "By this will we have been sanctified, through the offering of the body of Jesus Christ once and for all" (10:10). This verse's sacrificial terminology reminds us of Christ's correspondence to the Old Testament sacrifices. He is offered like a sacrifice to sanctify us.[10] Yet "once and for all" reminds us of the previous verses, where Christ is presented as the perfect fulfillment or goal to which the sacrifices pointed. Unlike the other sacrifices, Christ was only offered once (9:25-28).

It is easy to overlook the David typology undergirding Hebrews 10:5-10 and to focus instead on the sacrificial typology. Yet David typology is vital here, because it provides the force behind the quotation from Psalm 40:6-8. The author has anticipated his appeal to David typology by consistently referring to Jesus only as "Christ" in Hebrews 9:11, 14, 24, 28. Jesus and the New Testament writers regularly show that the Christ or Messiah is the antitype to David. The more obvious examples occur when the New Testament writers claim that Jesus fulfills a verse from a Psalm of David in which David is clearly speaking about himself.[11] With a few exceptions, they usually do not draw attention to the connection between the Psalm and David.[12] In most cases, David's experiences are predicting the suffering of Christ.[13] Therefore, the reader is usually expected to recognize the David typology that justifies the claim that Jesus fulfills a certain verse from a Psalm of David. This is what is going on in Hebrews 10:5-10.

When one looks at Psalm 40, one realizes that David is speaking about himself, especially in light of David's mention of his sins (40:12). Psalm 40:6-8 is not a direct prophecy concerning Christ, rather it is a typological prophecy.[14] As the type for Christ, David is making a claim about the Old Testament sacrifices. A similar claim is found in several places in the Old Testament.[15] Compared to similar claims from other authors, David's words are uniquely appropriate to predict the Christ's words about the sacrifices, because of the typological relationship between David and Christ. As the type for Christ, David's words about the sacrifices anticipate what the Christ will say about them. Without an understanding of David typology, one might not recognize that the words from Psalm 40:6-8 are viewed as prophetic or how they could be viewed as prophetic.

Table 6: Sacrificial Types and Antitypes in Hebrews 10	
Old Testament Type	**Antitype or Fulfillment in Sacrificial Death of Christ**
Reminder of Sins: Under the old covenant, the Day of Atonement sacrifices provide a yearly reminder of sins rather than taking away sins. (Heb. 10:1-4, Lev. 16)	Forgiveness of Sins: Christ offers himself as the ultimate sacrifice for sins. As a result, the new covenant people of God are forgiven of their sins. God does not remember them any more, so his people no longer need a yearly reminder of sins. (Heb. 10:5-18, Jer. 31:33-34)
David's Obedience: In Ps. 40:6-8, David speaks about the priority of doing God's will over offering the sacrifices. God desires obedience more than the sacrifices.	Christ's Obedience: Christ speaks David's words and fulfills them. Christ does God's will when he obediently offers his body as the fulfillment of the Old Testament sacrifices. (Heb. 10:6-10)
Repeatedly Offering Sacrifices: The priests are always standing to offer the same sacrifices over and over. These sacrifices do not take away sins. (Heb. 10:11)	Offering One Perfect Sacrifice: Christ offers one perfect sacrifice for sins and sits down at the right hand of God. His sacrifice perfects his people. No further sacrifice is necessary. (Heb. 10:12-18)

An unresolved and pressing question remains. The author of Hebrews introduces the quotation from Psalm 40 with "he says" (10:5). Just because the type said something, can one go on to assume that the antitype must have said something similar? Of course not. The author of Hebrews must think that Jesus actually did say these words or something very similar. We do not find this exact quotation anywhere in the Gospels, but Jesus does say similar things there. For instance, in comparison to Hebrews 10:5a and 10:6, Jesus does quote Hosea 6:6, when he says, "I desire mercy and not sacrifice" (Matthew 9:13, 12:7). Hosea 6:6 is one of the Old Testament verses that remind God's people that offering obedience to God is preferable to offering sacrifices. In Mark 12:33, a scribe interprets Jesus to mean that obedience to God's two greatest commandments is more important than offering sacrifices. In comparison to 10:5b, Jesus speaks about his sacrificial death in terms of giving his body for others (Luke 22:19, John 6:51).

In comparison to 10:7, Jesus elsewhere says that he has come to do God's will (John 4:34, 6:38). He includes his sacrificial death in God's will for him. For instance, Jesus says that the Father has commanded him to lay down his life for the sheep (John 10:15-18). He also voices his commitment to doing God's will in the Garden of Gethsemane just prior to his death (Matthew 26:42, Luke 22:42). In light of parallels like these, the author of Hebrews has reasonable grounds for saying that Christ said what David said in Psalm 40:6-8, even if he did not say those exact words. The author's interpretation of Psalm 40:6-8 is also justified, because Jesus similarly connected God's will for him with his death, which he described in terms of the sacrifice of his body for others.

One goal of this discussion has been to introduce David typology and its importance for Hebrews 10:5-10. As we saw in chapter two, David typology is very important for predicting the death of Christ. We usually do not think of David as predicting Christ's fulfillment of the Old Testament sacrifices through sacrificing himself. Yet this is where the author of Hebrews takes us as we follow his line of thinking through Hebrews 10:5-10. Having shown us that David foretells Christ's sacrifice, the author will next show us that David foretells some important things about Christ's role as priest.

David Predicts That Christ Will Be Greater Than the Old Testament Priests (Hebrews 10:11-14)

In Hebrews 10:11-14, the author directs our attention to the typological relationship between Christ and the Old Testament priests. He has done this in chapter 9 in relation to the High Priest. Now, he makes a few comments that show Christ to be greater than the priests as a whole, including the High Priest. The author makes his point in this case based upon allusions to Psalm 110, which is another psalm of David. Christ's fulfillment of Psalm 110:1 means that he is sitting down in the True Tabernacle. This makes him greater than the Old Testament priests, who stand daily in the Tabernacle to offer the same sacrifices. As was the case with the sacrifice itself (10:5-10), the reality is greater than the shadow contained in the Law (10:1).

The author sketches the picture of the type in Hebrews 10:11. At the end of the verse, he says some familiar things about the sacrifices. Every priest "repeatedly offers the same sacrifices, which are never able to take away sins" (10:11). The new point here is in the first words of the verse. "Every priest is standing daily, as he is serving." The author of Hebrews appears to be alluding to statements in Deuteronomy. Moses twice describes the priests as standing to serve the Lord or to minister (17:12, 18:5).[16] Similarly, Ezekiel also describes the priests as standing before the Lord to offer sacrifices (44:15).

In contrast, Christ offered "one sacrifice for sins for all time" and then "sat down at the right hand of God" (10:12). Not only did he sit down, but 10:13 implies that he continues sitting. He sat down and he "has been waiting from then on, until his enemies would be made a footstool for his feet" (10:13). What is the basis for the author's claim that Christ "sat down at the right hand of God" and remains sitting "until his enemies would be made his footstool"? The author is alluding to Psalm 110:1, which he is following closely here and has quoted in Hebrews 1:13. Psalm 110:1 says, "The LORD says to my Lord: 'Sit at My right hand until I make Your enemies a footstool for Your feet'" (NASB). Jesus alludes to Psalm 110:1 when he predicts his exaltation (Matthew 26:64, Mark 14:62, Luke 22:69). Peter also cites Psalm 110:1 as predicting Christ's exaltation to the right hand of God (Acts 2:33-36). Similarly, the author of Hebrews believes that Psalm 110:1 predicts Christ's exaltation to sit at the right hand of God, where he will remain until his enemies are brought into subjection to him (Hebrews 10:13).

Hebrews 10:14 then shows why it is right for Christ to sit down, and remain seated. Christ's perfect sacrifice is his "one offering" by which he "has perfected for all time the ones who are sanctified" (10:14). Since he has offered such a definitive sacrifice with such complete effects on the people of God, it is obvious that he does not need to stand in order to offer further sacrifices.

Based on the Scriptures, then, the author of Hebrews is pointing out a key difference between the Old Testament priests and the Christ that rests upon a typological relationship between them as priests of God. According to the Old Testament, priests must stand in the Tabernacle as they serve there, which includes offering sacrifices. If this is true for the type, then it should be true for the antitype as well. Therefore, in order to offer sacrifices in the True Tabernacle, one would expect Christ, like the Old Testament priests, to stand before the Lord in order to serve him and offer sacrifices there.[17] After all, Christ is a "priest forever in the order of Melchizedek" (7:17, Psalm 110:4) and a "servant" in the True Tabernacle (8:2). According to David's words in Psalm 110:1, Christ is sitting, not standing. Nor does Christ rise from his sitting position to offer any more sacrifices. He sits until God places his enemies under his feet in line once again with Psalm 110:1.

The fact that Christ sits down and remains seated is very important for the author of Hebrews. It provides one more piece of evidence that Christ has offered a perfect sacrifice that never needs to be repeated. Having offered such a sacrifice, he never needs to stand and offer another one. His sitting sets him apart as the antitype to the Old Testament priests. In other words, one knows that the priest in the order of Melchizedek (Psalm 110:4) is greater than the priests from the tribe of Levi, because he completes his priestly duty of offering sacrifices by offering one perfect sacrifice. God honors the superior priest by telling him to sit at his right hand (Psalm 110:1).

According to Hebrews 10:11-14, David predicted that Jesus would be a superior priest who would offer a better sacrifice. Our focus on David typology in relation to Psalm 40:6-8 means that we should look more closely at Psalm 110:1. Is this another instance of David typology? Delitzsch, among others, claims that Psalm 110 is a direct prophecy in which David speaks directly about the ultimate Messiah who is to come rather than about himself, Solomon, or other kings in his line.[18] This would make David typology unnecessary. Delitzsch regards Psalm 110 as a very unique case, which separates it from the numerous instances where Psalms of David should be interpreted typologically.

Others claim that Psalm 110 is not exclusively about the Messiah. It is possible for these words to be applicable in the first place to kings in the line of David, even if they are ultimately and completely fulfilled by the Messiah (the Christ).[19] In this case, Psalm 110 predicts Christ in a typological manner. This debate shows that it is sometimes difficult to distinguish between direct prophecy and typological prophecy. Psalm 110 and Psalm 2 are two of the difficult cases that are often cited in the New Testament. In both of these Psalms, and especially in Psalm 110, one finds language that Christ fulfills so much more completely than David's sons ever did. For instance, Christ is both fully king and fully priest forever, so that Psalm 110:4 fits him better than it fit any king before him (Hebrews 7:15-22).[20]

It seems likely that Psalm 110, like Psalm 2, makes a unique contribution to David typology. In these two psalms, David presents an inspired picture that God has revealed to him about God's anointed king.[21] In Psalm 110:1, he addresses God's king as "my lord," which is a title that David previously used in reference to two other kings.[22] When he calls God's king "my lord," David is acknowledging God's king as someone greater than himself. This sounds odd coming from David. God's king is supposed to be a son of David. How could David ever refer to one of his sons as his "lord"? "Lord" is a title for a superior, not a son. Jesus brings up this dilemma when he quotes Psalm 110:1 (Matthew 22:41-46).

First, we need to be sure that the anointed king of Psalm 110 is supposed to be a son of David. Is David addressing one of his sons as "lord"? We know that David expects one of his sons to be God's anointed king who will rule after him. In 2 Samuel 7:13, 16, God promises David to establish his throne and kingdom forever, which means that one of his sons will rule after him forever. Similarly, Psalm 110:4 mentions God's promise of an eternal priesthood for his anointed king. This priestly king rules from Zion, like David and his sons after him (Psalm 110:2, 2:6). If God keeps his promise to David, then the king of Psalm 110 should be a son of David who rules after him.

Why does David call one of his sons "lord"? The resolution to the tension probably lies in 2 Samuel 7:14 and Psalm 2:7. According to these verses, when a son of David becomes king, he becomes the son of God as well. In Psalm 2:7, God tells the king on the day of his anointing, "You are my son, today I have begotten you" (NASB). The king is no longer merely David's son. When he becomes king, David's son becomes God's son in a special way as well. As a result, when David writes Psalm 110 about the king at God's right hand, he rightly recognizes that this ruler will be God's king and not merely David's son. He rightly deserves to be addressed as "lord," even by David. This is probably what Jesus is trying to get the people to see when he quotes Psalm 110:1 in Matthew 22:41-46. The Messiah is no mere son of David. He is more than that.[23] He is the son of God. In the case of Jesus, the Messiah is truly the Son of God and much greater than David.

Therefore, in Psalm 110, David appears to be writing about the great kings who will rule after him.[24] It is important to notice that the king of Psalm 110 is not the beginning of the line of similar kings. Psalm 110 describes this king as being like David himself. For instance, David elsewhere talks about God dealing with his enemies in ways that are similar to Psalm 110 (Psalm 18:43-50).[25] Another psalmist makes similar claims about what God promised to David regarding his enemies (Psalm 89:19-29). On one level, then, in Psalm 110, David passes on to his sons an inspired picture of what it means to be a king like David.

On another level, Psalm 110, like Psalm 2, provides important hints that David and the similar kings who will follow him are pointing beyond themselves to something greater. In these psalms, David presents an ideal picture that captures what God has revealed to him about his rule and the rule of his sons after him. God has appointed David and his sons to be the "head of the nations" (18:43), so that God is the power behind their throne (2:6; 110:1, 5). It is therefore foolish for the kings of the earth to oppose these kings (2:10-11). God has promised the nations to them as their inheritance (2:8).[26] Interpreters have often noted that such language appears grandiose or extravagant. For instance, Gerhard von Rad says, "A petty Judean king was given in God's name a claim to world-wide domination and a saving office which he could not possibly fulfil."[27] David's inspired picture of himself as God's king over the nations may appear grandiose to us, because we know the full history that shows the limited extent to which David and his sons lived up to the inspired picture. Yet David did not know this history. He faithfully created an inspired picture of his great kingship and the greater kingship of his sons after him.

In doing so, David provides the type for the great king like David, the one who would come after him. Consequently, Psalm 110 and Psalm 2 are contributions to David typology, because they contribute to David's inspired picture of the great king like David. To refer back to this picture and predict its fulfillment, Ezekiel later mentions the name of David when he wants to talk about the king who is to come (Ezekiel 34:23-24, 37:24-25). [28] Micah also picks up on the importance of David as the type for the king who is to come. He predicts that the ruler like David will come from Bethlehem, where David came from (5:2, 1 Samuel 17:12). Like David, his greatness will extend to the "ends of the earth" (5:4). These direct prophecies point the way to the fulfillment of the typological picture created by David.

In fulfillment of David's typological picture, his perfect antitype is Jesus, the Christ. He fulfills David's words in ways that go beyond even David's great expectations. David probably was not envisioning one of his sons literally sitting in heaven at the right hand of God (Psalm 110:1, Hebrews 10:12).[29] Nor was he envisioning that one of his sons would rule over enemies far greater than merely mortal enemies, including spiritual powers and death itself (Hebrews 10:13, 1 Corinthians 15:24-27). David probably could not have adequately pictured how it would be possible for one of his sons to be both fully king and fully priest forever, so that Psalm 110:4 fits him so much better than it fit any king before him (Hebrews 7:15-22). Finally, David probably was not envisioning that the eternal Son of God would actually fulfill Psalm 110. Jesus truly was God's Son first and foremost, but a son of David as well (Romans 1:3).

It appears likely, then, that the use of Psalm 110:1 in Hebrews 10:11-14 is based on David typology, although it is not as straightforward as the David typology found in Hebrews 10:5-10. Jesus himself cited and alluded to this verse in Matthew, Mark, and Luke. His use of Psalm 110 accounts for the many references to this psalm in the New Testament.[30] Psalm 110 fits perfectly here in Hebrews 10, because it speaks about a figure who is both a king like David and a priest like Melchizedek. As priest, the Christ offers one perfect sacrifice and completes his priestly work of offering sacrifices. Then, as ruling king, he sits down at the right hand of God until God gives him complete victory over his enemies. As a result, Christ is able to fulfill both Old Testament types, namely, the priest and the king.

Complete Forgiveness Means that Sacrifices for Sin Are No Longer Necessary (Hebrews 10:15-18)

The author has just stated that Christ has offered the perfect sacrifice that sanctifies and perfects the people of God (10:10, 14). He now makes one more point that shows that sacrifices for sin are no longer necessary (10:15-18). They are no longer necessary, because Christ's sacrifice has secured complete forgiveness for sin (10:18). He shows this to be true based upon a quotation from Jeremiah 31:33-34. Hebrews 10:15-18 shows once again how the author of

Hebrews draws out the relationship between various typologies to show how they inform one another. In this case, he shows how Jeremiah's contribution to covenant typology teaches us something about the finality of Christ's sacrifice and the end of the Old Testament sacrifices.

Having shown how David typology implies the end of offering sacrifices for sin, the author returns to the covenant typology of Jeremiah 31, which he quoted from at length in Hebrews 8:8-12. Covenant typology also showed up in 9:15-20. In 10:16-17, he quotes selectively from Jeremiah 31:33-34. He prepares for the quotation from Jeremiah without any reference to Jeremiah. Rather, the Holy Spirit is given credit for speaking to us through these words from Jeremiah (10:15). Notice that the first quotation from Jeremiah is introduced with "for after he said" (10:15). This means that the first quotation (10:16) is included to prepare the way for the second quotation (10:17).

The first quotation introduces the future "covenant" (10:16). It begins to describe that covenant by saying, "I will put my laws upon their hearts and upon their minds I will write them" (Hebrews 10:16, Jeremiah 31:33). Then the author of Hebrews omits several lines to jump down to the relevant point for his purposes. The Holy Spirit says through Jeremiah, "And their sins and their lawless deeds I will certainly not remember ever again." On the basis of this point, he concludes, "Now where there is forgiveness for these (sins and lawless deeds), there is no longer an offering (or sacrifice) for sin" (10:18). In other words, full forgiveness means that no offering for sin is necessary. Now, it is interesting that he highlighted the promise not to remember their sins. Notice that he skipped over the immediately preceding phrase from Jeremiah 31:34, which says, "I will be merciful to their iniquities" (Hebrews 8:12). Why would remembering sins no more be more important for him?

The Old Testament speaks several times about God remembering his people's sins. When God remembers their sins, it is for the purpose of judgment (for example, Jeremiah 14:10, Hosea 8:13). Since God remembers sins, God's people need to remember their sins and seek his forgiveness and cleansing from sin. This is why they need the regular reminder of sins that the Day of Atonement provides (Hebrews 10:3). According to Jeremiah 31:34 (Hebrews 8:12, 10:17), the good news regarding the new covenant is that God will never remember their sins again. The author focuses on this statement, because it communicates a full and final remedy for sins. God does not remember sins that he has fully forgiven. If God has fully forgiven their sins, then God's people do not need to remember their sins every year and offer sacrifices for their sins on the Day of Atonement. This is what the author of Hebrews concludes in Hebrews 10:18. Thus, Hebrews 10:3 anticipates the point that is made in Hebrews 10:15-18.

God's ability to forgive sins and remember them no more is based upon the sacrifice of Jesus. In the Old Testament, God drew a strong connection between forgiveness of sin and sacrifice (Hebrews 9:22). It is therefore appropriate that 10:18 emphasizes forgiveness after discussing the sacrifice of Christ, which is the basis for that forgiveness (10:5-14).

Hebrews 10:18 is the conclusion that the author draws regarding the end of sacrifices. It implies that Christ's sacrifice is final and will not be repeated. It also implies that the Old Testament sacrifices for sin are no longer necessary. The one perfect sacrifice of Christ is their perfect antitype. The antitype fulfills the imperfect shadow contained in the Law (10:1). Like the Old Covenant, the Old Testament sacrifices are "obsolete" and are going to disappear (8:13).

Given our focus on typology, it is important to consider how Jeremiah 31:33-34 is distinct from Psalm 40:6-8 and Psalm 110:1. These psalms both relate in the first place to

David's picture of himself or of his sons who will be rulers like him. With respect to predicting Jesus, they are typological prophecies. They are predictive, because King David provides God's pattern for the great king who is to come. We know that King David provides God's pattern for the great king based on direct prophecies, like the ones cited in the previous section from Ezekiel and Micah. These direct prophecies point to King David as the pattern or type for the great king to come after him. In this way, they contribute to the David typology of the Old Testament.

Jeremiah 31:33-34, a direct prophecy, functions like these other direct prophecies by making a significant contribution to covenant typology. Jeremiah begins talking about a "new covenant" in 31:31. He refers back to the old covenant that God initiated after the Exodus from slavery in Egypt (31:32). Then, he talks about the new covenant in ways that are similar to, yet distinct from, the old covenant. For example, the new is like the old in that God's people will have his law. It is distinct in that God will write his law on the hearts of his people so that each one of them will know him (31:33-34). Jeremiah's description therefore shows that the new covenant stands in a typological relationship to the old. It is similar to the old covenant, but greater or more perfect in certain significant respects.

In Hebrews 10:15-18, the author focuses on what Jeremiah says about the new covenant's more perfect remedy for sin. In other words, he is focusing on a difference between the two covenants that shows the realities that come with the new covenant to be greater than the old covenant types. His use of Jeremiah 31:33-34 provides an important example of the contribution of direct prophecies to identifying and interpreting types in the Old Testament. Jeremiah 31's description of the new covenant, like Ezekiel 34's description of the new David, reveals that the old covenant is a type for a new and greater covenant. It provides some hints as to how the new covenant will be like and unlike the old covenant. Prophecies like Jeremiah 31 help us to read the Old Testament typologically. They reveal prominent Old Testament types and create expectations about their fulfillment. In the New Testament, we find the fulfillments of these types in their antitypes. In addition, we find fuller clarification regarding the nature of the antitypes. The antitypes often exceed the Old Testament expectations in certain respects, as we saw in the case of David above.

In the case of the new covenant, it focuses upon one sacrifice rather than many. The old covenant was inaugurated with "blood of the covenant" from sacrifices and associated with many subsequent sacrifices (Hebrews 9:18-22). The new covenant is also inaugurated with "blood of the covenant" from one perfect and final sacrifice for sin (10:18, 29). Jeremiah anticipates this greater aspect of the new covenant, when he says that God will no longer remember their sins. Only in light of the sacrifice of Christ does it become apparent just how God will provide the final and full remedy for sin that allows for the fulfillment of Jeremiah's expectation.

As you can see from the mention of "blood of the covenant," the significance of Jeremiah 31 in Hebrews 10:15-18 connects to the significance of the words of Jesus at the Last Supper. Jesus' words at the Last Supper also allude to Jeremiah 31's new covenant. He connects the new covenant to his blood and to forgiveness of sins (Luke 22:20, Matthew 26:28). It is quite helpful to study Hebrews 10:15-18 along with Jesus' words at the Last Supper regarding the new covenant (see chapter 3).

Let Us Draw Near to God for Priestly Service (Hebrews 10:19-22, 24-25)

The author now draws out some of the implications of his sacrificial typology for the life and service of believers

(Hebrews 10:19-25). The first implication is the most important for our purposes (10:19-22), because it focuses so clearly upon what Christ's fulfillment of the priesthood and sacrifices means for believers. Christ has opened up the way for believers to enter into the True Holy Place, God's True Tabernacle. The author does not call them priests, but he describes them like priests in 10:19-22. They are clearly the antitypes to the Old Testament priests, who were not able to enter the Holy of Holies on earth, much less God's True Holy Place in heaven. Let us look further at the benefits of being the new priests of the new covenant according to Hebrews 10:19-22.

It is important to notice the structure of Hebrews 10:19-22 before we look at the contents of these verses. These verses contain one central, main clause. The other clauses are all subordinate clauses that modify the main clause. By writing in this way, the author highlights the main idea of these verses. The main clause is "let us draw near with a true heart in full assurance of faith" (10:22a). The two subordinate clauses reveal why we can draw near to God in his True Holy Place.

The first subordinate clause is quite long, somewhat complex, and difficult to translate (10:19-21). It says something like this, "Therefore, brethren, since we have confidence for entering into the holy place by the blood of Jesus, and a new and living way through the veil (that is, by his flesh) that he inaugurated for us, and a great priest over the house of God" (10:19-21).[31] The clause names two benefits of Christ's perfect sacrifice (10:19-20) and then hints at the significance of having Christ as our priest over the house of God (10:21).

In terms of the benefits of Christ's perfect sacrifice, the author gives first place to believers' confidence for entering the True Holy Place in heaven. He is here stressing the fulfillment of the sacrifices of the Day of Atonement. On that day, the High Priest could enter the Holy of Holies with the blood of a sacrifice. Otherwise, entry meant death (Leviticus 16:2-3). As the antitype to these sacrifices, the blood of Jesus makes it possible for all believers to enter into the True Holy Place in heaven without fear of death. In other words, it gives them the confidence to enter the perfect Holy Place of God.

The next verse, 10:20, elaborates on the believers' access to God. It adds that believers have a "new and living way through the veil." This is in contrast to the situation under the old covenant. Before the new covenant, the way through the veil into the Holy of Holies was not yet revealed (9:8). Jesus had to inaugurate a "new" way through the veil "by his flesh." Hebrews 10:19 says that our entry into the True Holy Place is "by Jesus' blood." Why does the author change from blood in verse 19 to flesh in verse 20? One possible reason for the change is that blood and flesh are the two main elements of a sacrifice. Taken together, the mention of blood and flesh point to the death of Jesus as a sacrifice.

On the Day of Atonement, the High Priest who dares to enter through the veil does so with the blood of a sacrifice for his own sins and the sins of the priests (Leviticus 16:6). He also enters through the veil again on behalf of the people with a sacrifice for their sins (Leviticus 16:15). In neither case do these sacrifices open up the way for the High Priest, other priests, or the people to enter the Holy of Holies regularly and confidently. In contrast, the sacrifice of Jesus is the great antitype to the Day of Atonement sacrifices. This sacrifice opens up a "living" way into the Holy of Holies through the veil. It is a living way, because Jesus, the priest who opened the way, lives forever and guarantees that this way will always be open (7:25).[32]

Jesus also guarantees that this way will be effective, because he is our "great priest over the house of God" (10:21). The "house of God" in Hebrews is probably a reference to faithful believers, the people of God (Hebrews 3:6,

5:9).[33] It is therefore not surprising that the next verse exhorts believers to draw near "with a true heart" and "in full assurance of faith" (10:22a).

Hebrews 10:22b points to the new identity of God's people as his priests. Hebrews 10:22b, like 10:19-21, modifies "let us draw near" (10:22a). According to 10:22b, drawing near is possible "after we have had our hearts sprinkled from an evil conscience and our bodies washed with pure water."[34] At first glance, the author begins with a reference to familiar ground, namely, the internal cleansing of the conscience. We already know that the blood of Jesus cleanses the conscience (9:15). What about the sprinkling? Moses sprinkled all of the people with the blood of the covenant in Hebrews 9:19. Yet we find sprinkling coupled with washing of the body with water in 10:22b. The only other passing reference to washing the body or flesh with water occurred back in 9:10 with its reference to the "various washings" of the old covenant. What accounts for the author's sudden interest in the washing of the body? By now, we are accustomed to suspect that this has something to do with typology. In this case, he is describing believers as the antitypes to the Old Testament priests.

Washing the body with water and sprinkling with blood are found together in the Old Testament only when it talks about the sanctification of Aaron and his sons as priests (Exodus 29:4, 21; Leviticus 8:6, 30). Their sanctification prepares them to serve God as his priests. Similarly, in Hebrews 10:22, sprinkling with blood and washing with water prepares the priests of the new covenant to draw near to God.[35] As the antitypes to the old covenant priests, the priests of the new covenant benefit from a better sanctification. Through it, they are cleansed more thoroughly to remove sin and impurity from the conscience. As a result, they are able to draw near to God in his True Tabernacle.

The reference to the sanctification of the new priests in 10:22b suggests that we should review 10:19-21 for previous hints that believers are being viewed here as priests. In general, entry into the two rooms of the Tabernacle and drawing near to God are both special privileges of priests in the Old Testament. Recall that entry into the Holy of Holies through the veil is only permissible for the High Priest (9:7-8). Entry into the Holy Place, the first tent, is only permissible for priests (9:6). These limitations ensure that priests are able to draw nearer to God than is possible for non-priests. The Old Testament specifically says that only priests without physical blemishes can draw near to God to offer sacrifices at his altar (Leviticus 27:17-23, Ezekiel 44:16). Furthermore, they are the only ones who can draw near to the veil at the entrance to the Holy of Holies, where God dwells (Leviticus 21:23). In contrast to this, all of the new priests of the new covenant enter through the veil into the True Holy Place (Hebrews 10:19-20).

Just like the old covenant priests serve God under the High Priest, the new covenant priests also serve under a "great priest," Jesus (10:21). The reference to the cleansing of the conscience in 10:22 helps us to see how Hebrews 9:14 already anticipated that believers are new covenant priests. According to that verse, the blood of Christ cleanses the conscience of believers so that they can "serve the living God." Although it is hidden in most English translations, the only ones who "serve" God in Hebrews 9-10 are the priests who are constantly entering the Tabernacle to perform the "divine worship" or "divine service" (9:6).[36]

These points help us to focus on one of the great benefits of Christ's sacrifice for believers, namely, their ability to serve God as his priests. Hebrews 10:19-22 provides the picture of the fulfillment of the sacrifices and priesthood. This picture complements the picture of the corresponding Old Testament types back in 9:6-10. Comparing the two pictures reveals the benefits of the new covenant for believers. The perfect sacrifice of Christ provides the true remedy for sin that the old covenant sacrifices could not provide. His sacrifice sanctifies believers and they become perfect. As a result, they are in the proper condition to draw near to the holiness of God. All believers are priests under the new covenant whose access to God is far better than even the High Priest's access to God under the old covenant.

They are already able to draw near to God in his True Holy Place in heaven to offer up their sacrifices. These priests offer sacrifices, like praise, doing good, and sharing (13:15-16, 12:28). This is the type of priestly service that pleases God, namely, praise and obedient living. Therefore, the author of Hebrews exhorts believers to encourage each other to serve God faithfully through "love and good deeds" (10:24). They should gather together to present their sacrifices of praise to God and help one another to serve God faithfully (10:25).

Blessings of Priestly Service (Hebrews 4:16, 7:25, 10:23)

Serving God as his priests is truly a privilege and an honor. This is a great assignment. One of the great things about being God's servants is that God takes care of his own both now and forever. In Hebrews, we find two chief benefits of drawing near to God as his priests. First, God provides help for his servants in answer to their prayers and the prayers of Jesus on their behalf. Second, God rewards his servants. He promises to them an eternal inheritance (Hebrews 9:15).

While Hebrews 10:19-23 focuses our attention upon the privilege of being God's priests who can draw near to him, the attentive reader of Hebrews is able to associate this privilege with the benefits of drawing near to God. Jesus is the "great priest over the house of God" (10:21). Earlier, the author of Hebrews says something important about Jesus as

High Priest that is relevant here. As eternal High Priest, Jesus has the power to save "those who draw near to God through him," because he intercedes for them (7:25). The priests of God look to Jesus as their High Priest and benefit from his priesthood. He intercedes for them so that God would save them. What does salvation mean here? It probably means providing "help in time of need" (4:16). God's priests can confidently draw near to God's "throne of grace" to present their requests to God (4:16). They can expect to "receive mercy" and "find grace to help in time of need" (4:16). God hears his people and answers them.

Therefore, one of the benefits of drawing near to God in his True Tabernacle is that God answers the prayers of his priestly people. This is in keeping with one aspect of Tabernacle and Temple typology in the Old Testament. In several places, God's people are said to pray in, at, or toward the Temple or Tabernacle.[37] It is God's special dwelling place on earth and therefore the appropriate place to approach him with requests. God promises that his eyes and his heart are there (1 Kings 9:3). God says that it will one day be a "house of prayer for all nations" (Isaiah 56:7). In fulfillment of this, all believers are able to draw near to God in his True Tabernacle to present their requests to him in his true dwelling place. Believers already enjoy blessed communion with God through their access to his throne.

Even so, the author of Hebrews is aware that the life of believers requires endurance. In Hebrews 10:23, he says, "Let us keep on holding fast the confession of our hope without wavering; for the one who promised is faithful." The faithful God promises an eternal inheritance to his people (9:15). He is a God who rewards his faithful servants (10:35; 11:6, 26). In this world, God's servants endure trials of various kinds (Hebrews 10:32-34). Yet, by faith, they already see themselves as citizens of the "heavenly Jerusalem" (12:22). They are looking forward to the city that is to come (13:14). It is in that city that they will be able to enjoy the full benefits of the access to God that Christ's sacrifice has secured for them. As his servants, we are looking forward to the ultimate fulfillment of his promises in the New Jerusalem (Revelation 21:1-4). We will continue to serve him there and we will see his face (Revelation 22:1-5).

Reflection and Conclusion

Hebrews 8-10 provides a great opportunity to sample the typology that one finds in the New Testament. In these chapters, the author displays for us some of the important aspects of New Testament typology. We have seen how his points sometimes depend upon similarities between types and antitypes. What was true for the type must be true in some way for the antitype, because the type prefigures or predicts what is to come. He is also careful to point out how the fulfillment of the types means that the antitypes are the true realities that are greater than the types that preceded them. These observations regarding the relationship between types and antitypes in Hebrews are consistent with the author's teaching about the Law in Hebrews 10:1. The Law contains the "shadow of the good things to come" (10:1). Its sacrifices are never able to perfect the worshiper, only the one sacrifice of Christ can do that. Yet the sacrifices set forth in the Law are quite adequate for prefiguring the true sacrifice of Christ.

At the same time, Hebrews 8-10 provides us with another noteworthy aspect of New Testament typology. These chapters show how a variety of typological relationships are related in some important way to the sacrifice of Christ and the benefits that flow from it. In the preceding pages, we have touched on the typological significance of the Tabernacle/Temple, the priests, the sacrifices, David, and the old covenant. Understanding these typological relationships is generally helpful for understanding the work of Christ, because they are relationships that occur in other parts of the New Testament as well. They also illustrate one of the inspiring truths that typology brings to light. Studying the typology of the New Testament reveals a number of different Old Testament types that point to Christ and his work on the cross. The abundance of these types shows how abundantly God was predicting the climax of his saving work in Christ.

The focus of Hebrews 8-10 is the sacrificial death of Christ. I have seldom heard these passages preached or taught in church. They would seem to be great chapters to teach in conjunction with teaching about the Lord's Supper. They provide a fuller explication for some of the words of Jesus at the Last Supper. In particular, they develop Jesus' words about his blood, especially, "which is poured out for many for the forgiveness of sins" (Matthew 26:28). As seen in chapter three, these words point to Jesus' fulfillment of the Old Testament sacrifices of atonement. Hebrews 8-10 is the place to go for sustained teaching about Jesus' fulfillment of these sacrifices.

Hebrews 8-10 provides a good focal point for sustained reflection on the death of Jesus. As Christians, we chiefly think about Christ's sacrificial death at Easter. Building up to Easter and especially on Good Friday, we are likely to think about the significance of the death of Jesus. Hebrews 8-10 provides rich material to prepare us to present our sacrifices of praise to God for what he has done for us through the sacrificial death of his Son, the Christ.

Chapter 7

Conclusion

There is a lot to learn about the death of Jesus and a lot on which to meditate. I hope that the preceding chapters have illustrated this point. Christian teaching about the death of Jesus often relies heavily on the letters of Paul. It tends to glance quickly at the fulfillment of the Old Testament, as if the Old Testament does not provide much insight into the death of Jesus. We have seen the benefits of looking outside of Paul's writings, to the Gospels and Hebrews. At the same time, we have seen the benefits of attending to the fulfillment of the Old Testament.

The teaching of Jesus and the New Testament authors requires us to expand our understanding of fulfillment to include the fulfillment of types and typological prophecies. In chapter two, we encountered the important example of the Psalms of David in the Gospel of John. Jesus cites words of David and claims that he fulfills them (for example, John 13:18). John claims that Jesus fulfills words of David when he is suffering on the cross (John 19:24). When we examine David's words in their contexts, we discover that David appears to be writing about his own experiences. Yet we see indications in the Old Testament that David is the type for God's coming king. Jesus appears to be teaching that certain sufferings of David are typological sufferings. They predict the similar, yet greater, sufferings of Jesus, the great Son of David.

Our experience with David typology in John prepared us to see the fulfillment of types even where quotations are absent. In their accounts of the death of Jesus, Matthew, Mark, and Luke allude to some of the same words of David that John quoted. Matthew, Mark, and Luke are using allusions to point to Jesus' fulfillment of David's sufferings.

Appreciating the use of allusions to point to the fulfillment of types is vital for understanding the allusions in Jesus' words at the Last Supper. The compressed teaching in these words is expanded at various points in the New Testament. Jesus' words at the Last Supper allude to the fulfillment of the sacrifices of atonement, the blood of the covenant, and the fulfillment of the Passover. In chapter four, we examined the Gospel of John's significant treatment of the fulfillment of the Passover. John uses both quotations and allusions to tie the death of Jesus to the fulfillment of the Passover sacrifice. In chapters five and six, our focus was on sacrifices of atonement. Hebrews 9-10 concentrates our attention upon fulfillment of the sacrifices of the Day of Atonement. Along the way, the author brings in covenant typology and David typology to support his case.

When we look back over the preceding chapters, we can see the potential richness of a controlled use of typology. The New Testament contains plenty of quotations and allusions that point to typological relationships. It develops a satisfying variety of typological relationships and reveals the significance of each typological relationship for Christian theology. Important typological relationships get more attention and development.

Typology helps us to appreciate God's plan and his power. He directs historical events like the Passover to save his people and to predict their future salvation. He directs unbelieving soldiers to do his will, when they divide up Jesus' clothes and spare his legs from being broken. They unwittingly fulfill the words of David in the first case and the words of Moses in the second. David was writing about himself and Moses was writing about the Passover lamb. Centuries in advance, David's sufferings and the Passover sacrifice both prefigure the suffering and sacrifice of Jesus.

Part of God's plan included the writing of the Scriptures. They reveal his plan and his power for all to see. By revealing his plan in history and Scripture, God displays his unique power to rule over and foretell the course of history. Only God has this sort of control over history and insight into the future. As Isaiah 46:9-11 says,

> "Remember the former things long past,
> For I am God, and there is no other;
> I am God, and there is no one like Me,
> Declaring the end from the beginning,
> And from ancient times things which have not been done,
> Saying, 'My purpose will be established, And I will accomplish all My good pleasure';
> Calling a bird of prey from the east, The man of My purpose from a far country.
> Truly I have spoken; truly I will bring it to pass. I have planned it, surely I will do it" (NASB).

Endnotes

—ɯ—

Chapter 1
Setting the Course

[1] Much of this picture has been influenced by the helpful article by John Stek, "Biblical Typology Yesterday and Today" (see esp. 161-2). See the bibliography for the full bibliographic information for this work and for the works in the notes below.

[2] Aune describes the teleological view of history that is characteristic of the Old and New Testaments ("Early Christian Biblical Interpretation," 91-93, 95).

[3] Moo, "Sensus Plenior," 191; Moule, "Fulfillment-Words," 298-9, 314-5.

[4] Markus, "Presuppositions," 446-7; Dentan, "Typology," 215.

[5] A helpful article to provide guidance for detecting allusions is "Elusive Allusions: The Problematic Use of the Old Testament in Revelation" by Jon Paulien.

[6] Argyle, "Joseph the Patriarch in Patristic Teaching."

[7] Here and in the rest of the book, Greek terms are normally transliterated and placed in italics.

[8] Fee, *1 Corinthians*, 441-50; Davidson, *Typology*, 208-75.

[9] BDAG, s.v. *typos* and *typikōs*; Davidson, *Typology*, 286-90; Fritsch, "Biblical Typology" 104:88-90. BDAG is

an abbreviation for *A Greek-English Lexicon of the New Testament and Other Early Christian Literature*, revised and edited by F. Danker (Chicago: University of Chicago Press, 2000).

[10] The sentence structure of this verse is quite difficult in Greek. The best way to understand it is to take the initial relative clause as modifying "baptism" ("baptism, which is the antitype [to the salvation in the preceding verse], now also saves you"). On this verse, see Fritsch, *"TO ANTITYPON,"* 100-1; BDAG, s.v. *antitypos*; Davids, *1 Peter*, 143-5. Note the presence of "antitype" in Fritsch's translation and the New King James Version. Another possible translation for *antitypon* is "corresponds to" (English Standard Version).

[11] On the use of "shadow" in Hebrews 8:5, see chapter 5.

[12] Carson, *John*, 122.

[13] Brown, *John*, 501.

[14] Ladd, *Theology of the New Testament*, 303.

[15] The association between *alētheia* and antitypes leads ancient interpreters to read the movement from "Law" to "grace and truth" in John 1:17 in terms of movement from types (in the Law) to antitypes (the "truth" or "realities"). See, for instance, John Chrysostom, *Homilies on the Gospel of John* 14 (on John 1:17); Wiles, *The Spiritual Gospel*, 68-71.

[16] BDAG, s.v. *parabolē*.

[17] Even John Chrysostom notes that this is really typology rather than allegory (*Homilies on Galatians* at Galatians 4:24). Galatians 4:21-31 may be a further reason for Church Fathers to confuse typology and allegory. See also Ellis, *Paul's Use of the Old Testament*, 53-54; Goppelt, *Typos*, 139-40.

[18] Young, "Typology," 33; Brown, *Sensus Plenior*, 10.

[19] Indeed Frances Young says concerning the Church Fathers, "the supposed distinction between typology and allegory is far too fine a line to draw in practice: in most texts the one

shades into the other almost indistinguishably" ("Typology," 33).

[20] For example, see Justin, *Dialogue with Trypho*, chapter 90.

[21] See *From Shadows to Reality*, esp. 57-65.

[22] The *Epistle of Barnabas* provides a good example of the difference. Poor typology occurs in 9:7-8, where Abraham's circumcision of 318 men points to Jesus and the cross. Then, in chapter 10, one finds an allegorical interpretation of the food laws, where each forbidden animal represents a type of person or vice that one should avoid. Such an interpretation presents a deeper meaning that has nothing to do with prefiguring or predicting something later.

[23] On the internet, one can now find the full text of homilies/commentaries on the Gospel of John by important Church Fathers, like John Chrysostom, Cyril of Alexandria, and Augustine.

[24] *Protypōthen* is a form of the verb *protypoō*, which is a verb related to the noun *typos*. It is another word that some Church Fathers use as part of their vocabulary related to typology (Lampe, *Patristic Greek Lexicon*, s.v. *protypoō*).

[25] *On Pascha and Fragments*, ed. Stuart Hall (Oxford: Clarendon, 1979), 31 (lines 397-409).

[26] For more on typology in this homily, see T. F. Torrance, *Divine Meaning: Studies in Patristic Hermeneutics* (Edinburgh: T&T Clark, 1995), 79-81, 102-4.

[27] We will look further at this typology in chapter 4. It reflects the influence of the Gospel of John, especially John 8:31-47.

[28] *In dictum Pauli: Nolo vos ignorare* 247.61-248.12, 248.23-28. Translation taken from Jean Daniélou, *From Shadows to Reality*, 192, except for the words in brackets where I have introduced a few changes to bring it more in line with the Greek text.

Chapter 2
The Suffering of David Predicts the Suffering of Jesus the Christ

[1] Matthew 27:46/Mark 15:34; Luke 23:46; John 19:28.

[2] For example, see Ezekiel 34:23-24, 37:24-25. See also chapter 6.

[3] See also John 12:16, 20:9.

[4] Anticipation of the death of Jesus probably accounts for the change of verb tense from Psalm 69:9 ("has consumed") to the quote in John 2:17 ("will consume") (Bruce, *John*, 75).

[5] Keener, *John*, vol. 1, 528; Ridderbos, *John*, 116-7.

[6] Psalm 69 is attributed to David in its superscription and in Romans 11:9. Although Davidic authorship has been questioned in modern times, the New Testament supports Davidic authorship of several Psalms attributed to him (for example, Luke 20:42; Acts 1:16, 20; 2:25, 34-35) and even of one that is not clearly attributed to David (Acts 4:25-26).

[7] Carson, *John*, 180.

[8] As Herman Ridderbos observes, the translator must insert something between "but" and "so that," because the Greek sentence has left something out here (a case of ellipsis). In light of the next verse (13:19) and the parallels in 15:25 and 19:36, "it must happen" or "these things happen" is a likely insertion (*John*, 467).

[9] C. F. D. Moule treats several important aspects of the New Testament understanding of fulfillment ("Fulfilment-Words," 293-320).

[10] VanGemeren, *Psalms*, 327. Regarding the historical setting, see Delitzsch, *Psalms*, 306.

[11] See also D. A. Carson's comments on David typology in John 13:18 (*John*, 470).

[12] John 15:25 is similar to John 13:18 in that something must be supplied between "but" and "so that." See my note on the translation of 13:18 (above).

[13] See John 10:34 as well.

[14] As was the case with John 13:18 and 15:25, "these things happened" is inserted before "so that" to clarify how the verse fits together.

[15] See Carson, *John*, 620.

[16] Moo does a good of showing that this is preferable to the common tendency to see Jesus as fulfilling aspects of an unidentified "Righteous Sufferer" of the lament Psalms (*Old Testament*, 289-300).

[17] In Christian theology, it is common to refer to Jesus' suffering as the "passion" of Christ.

[18] *Matthew*, 575.

[19] Ibid. The reasoning in the preceding four sentences also comes from Carson.

[20] If one sees and values the connection between Matthew 27:34 and Psalm 69:21, then it becomes less likely that one will try to interpret this as a merciful action intended to dull Jesus' pain (see Moo, *Old Testament*, 250-1).

[21] Moo, *Old Testament*, 258. Besides Psalm 22:7, Moo provides some other analogous Old Testament examples like Lamentations 2:15, 2 Kings 19:21, Job 16:4, and Psalm 109:25.

[22] See Moo, *Old Testament*, 259.

[23] *Matthew*, 577.

[24] See Stott, *Cross of Christ*, 80-82 and Moo, *Old Testament*, 271-5 for several common approaches to understanding Matthew 27:46.

[25] VanGemeren, *Psalms*, 200.

[26] Delitzsch, *Psalms*, 195. Delitzsch also has some very helpful comments on the typological significance of Psalm 22 as a whole (*Psalms*, 193).

[27] Ibid., 195.

[28] Theologians often discuss what this means for the Trinity and its unity. C. E. B. Cranfield addresses this issue with some often-quoted words, "It is, of course, theologically important

to maintain the paradox that, while this God-forsakenness was utterly real, the unity of the Blessed Trinity was even then unbroken" (*Mark*, 459).

[29] It appears to be somewhat challenging to harmonize Matthew 27:47-49 and John 19:28-29 unless one allows that these are referring to two distinct events. It is possible that Jesus was given a drink in the first instance and later requested a drink in the second.

[30] See Morris, *New Testament Theology*, 213.

[31] Moo, *Old Testament*, 281; Delitzsch, *Psalms*, 246.

[32] Moo, *Old Testament*, 281; VanGemeren, *Psalms*, 264.

[33] Bock, *Luke*, 1862; Delitzsch, *Psalms*, 246.

[34] This point and the preceding are made by Bock, *Luke*, 1862.

[35] See ibid.

[36] Of course, Jesus was not suffering due to sin, like David was (Psalm 31:10).

[37] See Hengstenberg, *Psalms*, vol. 1, 358, 361.

Chapter 3
Jesus' Words at the Lord's Supper in Light of the Old Testament Sacrifices

The Hebrew verb is *kipper* (this is how it is often transliterated in theological works).

[2] Morris, *Apostolic Preaching*, 167.

[3] The Greek verb is *ekcheō* (see Genesis 9:6, Leviticus 4:7).

[4] See Hengel, *Atonement*, 49-54.

[5] Moo, *Old Testament*, 310-1.

[6] See Hengel, *Atonement*, 51, 53.

[7] Ibid., 50, 73.

[8] Ibid., 8, 59-60. See, for instance, Luke 22:37, Hebrews 9:28.

[9] Wenham, *Leviticus*, 26-27.

[10] Wenham, *Leviticus*, 22. The Old Testament does not explain what holiness really is, but it does indicate that holiness is something "intrinsic to God's character" (Ibid.).

[11] Some translations prefer the verb "to consecrate" instead.

[12] Wenham, *Leviticus*, 142.

[13] Ibid., 143.

[14] Kiuchi, *Purification Offering*, 95-99, 103.

[15] Dumbrell, *Covenant and Creation*, 94; Wenham, *Leviticus*, 26-27.

[16] See 1 Peter 1:22-25, where Peter calls Christians to obey the command to love their brothers, which comes from God's word.

[17] "This" (*touto*) is a neuter singular demonstrative pronoun with an action for its antecedent, because it is not logically feasible to single out a neuter noun in the sentence that could function as its antecedent.

[18] Fee, *1 Corinthians*, 551.

[19] Garland, *1 Corinthians*, 548.

[20] Fee, *1 Corinthians*, 540.

[21] When one looks at the Septuagint translation, one does not find the same Greek words for "remembrance" in Exodus 12:14 and Luke 22:20. In Greek and in English, though, the words are similar in meaning.

[22] Fee, *1 Corinthians*, 553.

Chapter 4
The Fulfillment of the Passover in the Gospel of John

Keil, *Pentateuch*, 297-8.

[2] Wenham, *Leviticus*, 78; see also 82, note 15.

[3] Alexander, "The Passover Sacrifice," 8. See Exodus 9:20 where Pharaoh's servants and animals flee into houses for protection from the hail.

[4] Wenham, *Leviticus*, 22.

[5] Alexander, "Passover Sacrifice," 8.

[6] Numbers 16:41-50, 25:7-13; see also Numbers 8:19, Exodus 30:11-16, 2 Samuel 24 (esp. 24:21), and 1 Chronicles 21 (esp. 21:22-27).

[7] Melito, *On Pascha*, sections 67-68; for other Church Fathers, see Hoskins, "Freedom from Slavery to Sin and the Devil," 1.

[8] John 8:31 says these Jews have believed in Jesus, but they are not true believers. By the end of the chapter, they have turned against Jesus. They are not the only examples of fickle faith in John.

[9] Ridderbos, *John*, 299.

Chapter 5
Hebrews 9: Entering into the True Tabernacle through the Blood of Jesus

See Psalms 84, 46, 48.

[2] It is notoriously difficult to translate *ta hagia* in this passage. As often as possible, I have translated it as either "Holy Place" or "Holy of Holies" rather than as "sanctuary" or other possibilities.

[3] Bruce, *Hebrews*, 198.

[4] Exodus 25:22; Numbers 7:89; 1 Samuel 4:4, 21-22; 2 Samuel 6:2; 2 Kings 19:15; Ezekiel 43:7.

[5] God is enthroned or dwells in heaven: Psalms 33:13-14, 102:19, 103:19, 113:5, 115:3, 123:1; Isaiah 66:1. The Tabernacle/Temple is his footstool: Psalm 99:5, Lamentations 2:1, Isaiah 66:1.

[6] The wording of this short description of the Tabernacle has caused a good bit of confusion among interpreters regarding its fit with the Old Testament. One can find a good treatment of the ambiguities in F. F. Bruce's commentary (*Hebrews*, 197-205).

[7] Although it is not apparent from translations, Hebrews 9:8 is a subordinate, adverbial clause that modifies the implied main verb ("enters") of 9:7. The clause contains an adverbial participle. It probably indicates God's intended purpose for the limited access of the High Priest. A helpful translation would look something like this: "only the high priest enters once a year . . . in order for the Holy Spirit to show this: the way into the Holy of Holies has not yet been revealed while the first tabernacle retains its status (as the Holy Place of God)."

[8] On Hebrews 9:10, I was influenced by the helpful translation found in Attridge, *Hebrews*, 230.

[9] John Chrysostom, *Homilies on Hebrews*, 15.

[10] Kiuchi, *Purification Offering*, 96-98.

[11] Harrington, "Clean and Unclean," *New Interpreter's Dictionary of the Bible*, vol. 1, 683, 688.

[12] Similarly, in Ezekiel 43:7-9, God criticizes his people for defiling his Temple through their sins and by placing the dead bodies of their kings too near to his holy Temple. They have therefore defiled his Temple with uncleanness arising from contact with death.

[13] See John Chrysostom, *Homilies on Hebrews*, 15 (on Hebrews 9:14).

[14] Attridge, *Hebrews*, 164.

[15] See Bruce, *Hebrews*, 218.

[16] Josephus, *Antiquities*, 3.206. Josephus is a first-century Jewish writer.

[17] Wenham, *Leviticus*, 232. The altar of incense in the Tabernacle is quite clearly supposed to be cleansed with blood on the Day of Atonement (Exodus 30:10).

[18] Delitzsch provides a good overview of the options considered by interpreters (*Hebrews*, vol. 2, 124-5).

[19] See Koester, *Hebrews*, 426; Lünemann, *Hebrews*, 623-4.

[20] Bruce, *Hebrews*, 228.

[21] See also the treatment of Hebrews 10:22b in the next chapter.

[22] See first section of this chapter.

Chapter 6
Hebrews 10: The Unique Sacrifice of the Messiah Takes away Sin

"Consciousness" is the correct translation for the same Greek word (*suneidēsis*) that is translated "conscience" in 9:9, 14. The conscience is the part of us responsible for keeping track of our moral choices and deeds. An "evil conscience" is one that is stained by consciousness of sins (10:22).

[2] Hughes, *Hebrews*, 392.

[3] Delitzsch, *Hebrews*, vol. 2, 150-4; see Bruce, *Hebrews*, 239. VanGemeren and Kraus also see this as a typological use of Psalm 40:6-8 (VanGemeren, *Psalms*, 321; Kraus, *Psalms 1-59*, 427).

[4] Logic seems to necessitate that he speaks these things, after he has come into the world and not while he is coming into the world. The Greek expression here is somewhat idiomatic and analogous to something we do in English as well. In Greek, the verse begins with a present tense adverbial participle that is probably temporal ("when he comes into"). The participle and main verb ("says") are both historical presents. The historical present is a common use of the present tense that one uses to talk about past events as if they were occurring in the present in order to make hearers feel more involved in the story. We sometimes say something like this, "When my teacher comes into the classroom, he says. . . ." We can understand the "when" clause with an historical present to occur at the same time as or before the main action ("says").

[5] Bruce, *Hebrews*, 240-1.

[6] Bruce, *Hebrews*, 240; Delitzsch, *Hebrews*, vol. 2, 153.

[7] Koester does a good job of showing where the author follows or departs from the Hebrew text and the Septuagint (*Hebrews*, Anchor Bible, 432). Of course, we must recognize the difficulty of knowing exactly what Greek and Hebrew texts the author has access to and what readings those texts contain.

[8] Attridge, *Hebrews*, 275-6; Bruce, *Hebrews*, 242; Hughes, *Hebrews*, 399.

[9] Leon Morris, *The Cross in the New Testament*, 295-6; James Denney, *The Death of Christ* (1911), 169-70.

[10] See John 17:19.

[11] For example, Jesus claims that his betrayal by Judas fulfills Psalm 41:9 (John 13:18). Similarly, Peter claims that Judas's death fulfills Psalm 109:8 (Acts 1:20). See chapter 2 above.

[12] See exceptions in Acts 1:16, 20; 2:25-32.

[13] This is especially true of the many references to Psalms 22 and 69.

[14] Delitzsch, *Hebrews*, vol. 2, 152-4.

[15] 1 Samuel 15:22; Psalm 51:14-17; Isaiah 1:11-18, 66:1-4; Jeremiah 7:21-23; Hosea 6:4-6; Amos 5:21-24; Micah 6:6-8 (Bruce, *Hebrews*, 238).

[16] See the wording in the Septuagint. Delitzsch, *Hebrews*, vol. 2, 159; Hughes, *Hebrews*, 400.

[17] Delitzsch, *Hebrews*, vol. 2, 161.

[18] Delitzsch, *Psalms*, 691-4. See also Delitzsch, *Hebrews*, vol. 1, 85-92; Bateman, "Psalm 110:1," 445-7; John Calvin's commentary on the Psalms at Psalm 110.

[19] VanGemeren, *Psalms*, 696-9. See also Kraus, *Psalms 60-150*, 353-4.

[20] Note the limited priestly roles of David and Solomon (VanGemeren, *Psalms*, 699).

[21] David also wrote Psalm 2 according to Acts 4:25.

[22] Saul (for example, 1 Samuel 24:6) and Achish (1 Samuel 29:8). Bateman, "Psalm 110:1," 449.

[23] Carson, *Matthew*, 468.

[24] Delitzsch, *Psalms*, 693.

[25] See also 2 Samuel 7:9-11. Delitzsch mentions specific historical events in which David experienced victory over enemies (*Psalms*, 693).

[26] Solomon says similar things about himself in Psalm 72:8-11.

[27] *Old Testament Theology*, vol. 2, 374.

[28] See also Isaiah 9:6-7 and the yearning for fulfillment in Psalm 89.

[29] See Bateman, "Psalm 110:1," 451.

[30] Carson, *Matthew*, 468. Jesus' citation: Matthew 22:41-46, Mark 12:35-37, Luke 20:41-44; allusion: Matthew 26:64, Mark 14:62, Luke 22:69.

[31] See especially the similar translation in Koester, *Hebrews*, 442.

[32] Bruce, *Hebrews*, 250.

[33] It is significant that Jesus is "over the house of God." In Hebrews 8:8-10, God's new covenant is with the "house of Israel" and the "house of Judah." By using the term "house of God" instead, the author stresses faithfulness to God as the key mark of the new covenant people of God (see 3:6, 5:9).

[34] Regarding the translation, see Bruce, *Hebrews*, 248, note 79.

[35] Moffatt, *Hebrews*, 144-5; Delitzsch, *Hebrews*, vol. 2, 176-9.

[36] Forms of the verb *latreuō* ("serve" or "worship") occur in 9:9, 14; 10:2. The related noun *latreia* ("service" or "worship") occurs in 9:6.

[37] 1 Kings 8:29-30, 33, 35, 38, 42, 44, 47; Psalm 18:6, 28:2; 1 Samuel 1:10-12.

Appendix 1:

Glossary

—⚏—

Antitype. In writings on typology, antitype refers to a New Testament event, person, or institution that fulfills an Old Testament type. The antitype possesses significant similarities to its type. As the fulfillment or goal of the imperfect type, the antitype will be greater than the type that anticipated it. The term comes from the Greek word *antitypon* (etymology: *anti + typos*, meaning corresponding to a type or pattern). 1 Peter 3:21 uses the word *antitypon* in a way that probably lies behind the popular use of the term "antitype" in writings on typology.

Atonement. In biblical theology, atonement has to do with reconciliation between God and man. Reconciliation is necessary, because sin alienates man from God. In the Old Testament, atonement or making atonement is generally associated with offering sacrifices. In the New Testament, Jesus' sacrificial death is the ultimate and final sacrifice of atonement that reconciles God and man.

Church Fathers refers to the early teachers of the church in the first four or five centuries after the writers of the New Testament.

Direct prophecy is a term used in this book to indicate an Old Testament prophecy that appears to be a straightforward prediction of its New Testament fulfillment. When one studies a direct prophecy in its Old Testament context, one can see that it appears to be predicting something in the future. Also, when the New Testament quotes or alludes to this prophecy, the fulfillment seems to be in line with what was predicted. In other words, understanding the fulfillment does not depend upon detecting a relationship between a type and its antitype. Even so, direct prophecies can contribute to typology by predicting the fulfillment of Old Testament types, like David (Ezekiel 34:23) or the covenant (Jeremiah 31:31-34). See typological prophecy.

Holy describes "anyone or anything given to God." A holy person is "dedicated to the service of God." Generally, a person or thing becomes holy through sanctification (Wenham, *Leviticus*, 22). See sanctify.

LXX. A common abbreviation for the Septuagint. See Septuagint.

Passion. In Christian theology, it is common to refer to Jesus' suffering as the "passion" of Christ.

Redemption. In biblical theology, redemption involves freeing God's people from bondage to someone or something that has power over them. In the Old Testament, the most famous example of redemption occurs when God frees his people from Pharaoh and the Egyptians. Corresponding to this, Jesus frees believers from slavery to sin and the devil. Redemption ordinarily involves paying a price to free someone from bondage. Although the Bible uses redemption language in Exodus and the New Testament, God does not pay Pharaoh or the devil anything to set his people free. For more on this, see the first section of chapter 4 regarding the Passover.

Sanctify. In Exodus and Leviticus, to sanctify someone or something means to make someone or something holy. Sanctification often takes place through the blood of sacrifices (Wenham, *Leviticus*, 23). See holy.

Septuagint. The Septuagint refers to the Greek translation of the Old Testament that Jews (and Christians) used in the first century. We do not have a complete copy of the Septuagint translation that dates to the first century or before. We also have to remember that the Septuagint was still being copied by hand in the first century, so differences would have existed among various copies. So, when we are talking about the "Septuagint," we are really referring to our best reconstruction of the Greek translation of the Old Testament that would have been in use in the time of Jesus and the apostles. LXX is a common abbreviation for the Septuagint.

Shadow is often used to refer to Old Testament types. It points to the imperfection of types in comparison to the antitypes that cast the shadow. This usage of "shadow" arises from Hebrews 10:1 and Colossians 2:17, which basically say that the Old Testament Law contains the shadow of the things which are to come (see chapter 1).

Type. An Old Testament event (like the Exodus), person (like David), or institution (like the Temple) that prefigures a corresponding New Testament antitype or fulfillment.

Typology is the aspect of biblical interpretation that treats the significance of Old Testament types for prefiguring corresponding New Testament antitypes or fulfillments.

Typological prophecy is a term used in this book to indicate cases where the fulfillment of prophecy has to do with the fulfillment of a type by its antitype. Instances of typological prophecy generally become apparent to the reader of the New Testament as a result of looking back at the Old Testament context of quotations from or allusions to the Old Testament. When you look at the Old Testament context, you will find there a story, statement, or description that has to do with an event, person, or institution in the history of God's people. In other words, the Old Testament passage will normally appear to have more to do with some aspect of Israel's history than with prophecy regarding the future of God's people. A good example of typological prophecy is Jesus' claim to fulfill Psalm 41:9 (John 13:18). See direct prophecy.

Appendix 2:

How to Use this Book (for Ministers and Teachers)

—ᴍᴍ—

I have written this book to help a variety of readers to understand the New Testament better. I would like to think that ministers and teachers would find this book to be useful for teaching Christians about the Lord's Supper, Easter, and Passover. I would like to say a few words about how this book might be helpful for preaching or teaching on each of these topics.

1. Lord's Supper. Chapters 2 through 6 have to do with the sacrificial death of Christ. There is a lot of material in these chapters that could provide the substance for teaching at the Lord's Supper. In particular, chapters 3 and 4 provide many points of connection with the words of Jesus that we say at the Lord's Supper. It would be best to divide this teaching into smaller units that could inform a short sermon (or Bible study) in preparation for the Lord's Supper. For instance, the first section of chapter 3 might provide material for a short sermon on the sacrifices of atonement in relation to the words of Jesus at the Last Supper. Another short sermon on Isaiah 53 could be developed from this same section. Similarly, one or two sermons could be developed based on each section of this chapter. In this way, someone could teach slowly and carefully through the words of Jesus at the Last Supper. Chapter 4 would also lend itself to teaching in preparation for the Lord's Supper. For instance, chapter 4 explains John 6:51-58, where Jesus speaks about the benefits of eating his flesh and drinking his blood.

2. Easter. Ministers and teachers often tend to focus on the events of the death of Jesus without teaching a lot about the significance of the death of Jesus. In this book, I have shown a number of instances where Jesus and the apostles teach us about the significance of the death of Jesus. Many Christians can claim that Jesus died for their sins, but they do not grasp the significance of forgiveness of sins. Forgiveness of sins is vital for reconciliation to God and drawing near to God for priestly service (Hebrews 9-10). Reconciliation to God through Christ's sacrifice of atonement must occur in order for us to become God's holy people. When we become God's holy people through the sanctifying power of Christ's blood, God redeems us from the powers that hold us in bondage so that we can serve him and him alone. Atonement, sanctification, and redemption are rich, biblical themes that we can preach and teach at Easter time. They help us to teach the message of the Gospel in its biblical context.

How could this book help? Chapters 2 through 4 of this book would each lend themselves to an Easter sermon series (or series of Bible studies). Chapters 5 and 6 might be combined into one sermon series. By proceeding in this way, you could deepen your people's understanding of the significance of the death of Christ over the course of 4 or more years.

3. Passover. Christian celebrations of Passover have become more common in recent years. Chapters 3 and 4 would be especially helpful in these settings. During and after the Passover meal, Christians often struggle to relate the Passover to the death of Jesus. When I have celebrated the Passover with my family, I bring out the significance of the death of Jesus after dinner in association with the third cup of the Passover, which is the cup of redemption. I explain how Jesus fulfills the Passover by dying at Passover time to deliver us from death and to redeem us from slavery to sin and the devil.

Appendix 3:

Lent/Easter Readings

—⁂—

One of the ways that I have used the material in this book is to provide readings for my church to prepare people for Easter. I have used the readings below a few times. It would be quite possible to come up with additional or alternative readings based on the chapters above. Another possible theme for a week would be the theme of covenant and new covenant, which I have touched on at several points above. A week of readings related to Christ's fulfillment of David typology would also be quite easy to construct based on chapter 2.

Week 1 – Atonement: Jesus, the Lamb of God, Reconciles Us to God by Dying So That Ours Sins Could Be Forgiven	
Sunday	Leviticus 4:13-21, 27-31; Leviticus 17:10-11
Monday	Leviticus 16
Tuesday	Hebrews 9:1-14
Wednesday	Hebrews 9:15-28
Thursday	Hebrews 10:1-10
Friday	Hebrews 10:11-25
Saturday	John 1:29, 1 John 1:5-2:2
Week 2 – Redemption: The Lamb of God Died to Set Us Free from Slavery to Sin and the Devil	
Sunday	Exodus 12:1-22
Monday	Exodus 12:23-51
Tuesday	John 8:31-47
Wednesday	1 Peter 1:17-21
Thursday	Romans 6
Friday	Ephesians 2:1-3, Colossians 1:13-14
Saturday	Revelation 1:4-6, 5:1-14
Week 3 – The Death of the Lamb of God, Our Sacrifice of Atonement and Redemption	
Sunday	John 12:12-36
Monday	Mark 8:27-33, 9:30-32, 10:32-34
Tuesday	John 12:37-50
Wednesday	John 13 and Matthew 26:26-30
Thursday	John 18 and Luke 22:39-46
Friday	John 19
Saturday	Matthew 27:11-66
Sunday	John 20

Appendix 4:

Books for Further Reading

—⁓—

Beale, G. K. and D. A. Carson, eds. *Commentary on the New Testament Use of the Old Testament.* Grand Rapids: Baker, 2007.
This is a comprehensive survey of the use of the Old Testament in the New Testament. It is a scholarly work that repays careful reading.

Goppelt, Leonhard. *Typos: The Typological Interpretation of the Old Testament in the New.* Translated by D. H. Madvig. Grand Rapids: Eerdmans, 1982.
This is one of the most widely regarded scholarly treatments of typology done in the last 100 years. It provides a survey of a number of typological relationships.

Marshall, I. Howard. *The Work of Christ.* Carlisle, UK: Paternoster Press, 1969.
This is a great introduction to the significance of the death of Christ. It is accessible and short, but full of worthwhile insights.

Melito, Bishop of Sardis. *On Pascha and Fragments*. Edited by Stuart George Hall. Oxford: Clarendon Press, 1979.

This is a second-century sermon preached at Passover time. It is one of our earliest records of how Christians celebrated Passover. It provides a good example of how to teach about the fulfillment of the Passover. A note of caution: Some of his comments are very critical of Jews, probably due to tensions between Christians and Jews at that time.

Morris, Leon. *The Atonement: Its Meaning and Significance*. Downers Grove: InterVarsity Press, 1983.

This is a classic work of New Testament theology that focuses on the death of Christ. It does a good job of relating the New Testament teaching to the Old Testament. Morris is known for his writings on the cross, and this is one of his more accessible works.

Stott, John R. W. *The Cross of Christ*. Downers Grove: InterVarsity, 1986.

It provides a good overview of the theology of the death of Christ and does a good job of helping the reader to think about the implications of the death of Christ for Christian living.

Tidball, Derek. *The Message of the Cross*. The Bible Speaks Today. Downers Grove: InterVarsity, 2001.

The major advantage of this work is that it focuses on major passages from the Bible related to the death of Christ. Its goal is to help the reader to teach or preach about the death of Christ.

Bibliography

—⟡—

Alexander, T. Desmond. "The Passover Sacrifice." Pages 1-24 in *Sacrifice in the Bible*. Edited by Roger T. Beckwith and Martin J. Selman. Grand Rapids: Baker Book House, 1995.

Argyle, A.W. "Joseph the Patriarch in Patristic Teaching." *Expository Times* 67 (1955-56): 199-201.

Attridge, Harold W. *The Epistle to the Hebrews: A Commentary on the Epistle to the Hebrews*. Hermeneia. Philadelphia: Fortress Press, 1989.

Aune, David E. "Early Christian Biblical Interpretation." *Evangelical Quarterly* 41 (1969): 89-96.

Bateman, Herbert W. IV. "Psalm 110:1 and the New Testament." *Bibliotheca Sacra* 149 (1992): 438-53.

Bock, Darrell L. *Luke, Volume 2: 9:51-24:53*. Baker Exegetical Commentary on the New Testament. Grand Rapids: Baker, 1996.

Brown, Raymond E. *The Gospel according to John I-XII*. Anchor Bible, vol. 29. New York: Doubleday, 1966.

_____. The *Sensus Plenior* of Sacred Scripture. Baltimore: Saint Mary's University, 1955.

Bruce, F. F. *The Epistle to the Hebrews*. Rev. ed. New International Commentary on the New Testament. Grand Rapids: Eerdmans, 1990.

_____. *The Gospel of John: Introduction, Exposition and Notes*. Grand Rapids: Eerdmans, 1983.

Calvin, John. *Commentary on the Book of Psalms*. Vol. 4. Translated by James Anderson. Grand Rapids: Eerdmans, 1959.

Carson, D. A. *The Gospel according to John*. Grand Rapids: Eerdmans, 1991.

_____. "Matthew." In *The Expositor's Bible Commentary*, vol. 8. Grand Rapids: Zondervan, 1995.

Chrysostom, John. *Saint Chrysostom: Homilies on the Gospel of St. John and the Epistle to the Hebrews*. A Select Library of the Nicene and Post-Nicene Fathers of the Christian Church, 1st series, vol. 14. Grand Rapids: Eerdmans, 1983.

Cranfield, C.E.B. *The Gospel According to Saint Mark: an Introduction and Commentary*. Cambridge Greek Testament Commentary. Cambridge: Cambridge University Press, 1959.

Daniélou, Jean. *From Shadows to Reality: Studies in the Biblical Typology of the Fathers*. Translated by W. Hibberd. London: Burns and Oates, 1960.

Davids, Peter. *The First Epistle of Peter*. New International Commentary on the New Testament. Grand Rapids: Eerdmans, 1990.

Davidson, Richard M. *Typology in Scripture: A Study of Hermeneutical Typos Structures*. Berrien Springs, MI: Andrews University Press, 1981.

Delitzsch, Franz. *Psalms*. Translated by Francis Bolton. Commentary on the Old Testament, vol. 5. Peabody, MA: Hendrickson, 2006.

_____. *Commentary on the Epistle to the Hebrews*. 2 vols. Translated by T. Kingsbury. Minneapolis: Klock and Klock Christian Publishers, 1978.

Denney, James. *The Death of Christ*. Rev. ed. London: Hodder and Stoughton, 1911.

Dumbrell, William J. *Covenant and Creation: A Theology of Old Testament Covenants*. Nashville: Thomas Nelson, 1984.

Ellis, E. Earle. *Paul's Use of the Old Testament*. Grand Rapids: Eerdmans, 1957.

Fee, Gordon. *The First Epistle to the Corinthians*. New International Commentary on the New Testament. Grand Rapids: Eerdmans, 1987.

Fritsch, Charles T. "Biblical Typology." *Bibliotheca Sacra* 104 (1947): 87-100, 214-22.

_____. *"TO ANTITYPON."* Pages 100-107 in *Studia Biblica et Semitica*. Wageningen: H. Veenman and Zonen N. V., 1966.

Garland, David E. *1 Corinthians*. Baker Exegetical Commentary on the New Testament. Grand Rapids: Baker Academic, 2003.

Goppelt, Leonhard. *Typos: The Typological Interpretation of the Old Testament in the New*. Translated by D. H. Madvig. Grand Rapids: Eerdmans, 1982.

Harrington, Hannah K. "Clean and Uncelan." Pages 681-9 in *New Interpreter's Dictionary of the Bible*, vol. 1. Nashville: Abingdon, 2006.

Hengel, Martin. *The Atonement: The Origins of the Doctrine in the New Testament*. Translated by John Bowden. Philadelphia: Fortress Press, 1981.

Hengstenberg, E. W. *Commentary on the Psalms*. Translated by J. Thomson and P. Fairbairn. Edinburgh: T&T Clark, 1860.

Hoskins, Paul M. *Jesus as the Fulfillment of the Temple in the Gospel of John*. Paternoster Biblical Monographs. Milton Keynes, UK: Paternoster, 2006.

_____. "Deliverance from Death by the True Passover Lamb: A Significant Aspect of the Fulfillment of the Passover in the Gospel of John." *Journal of the Evangelical Theological Society* 52 (2009): 285-300.

_____. "Freedom from Slavery to Sin and the Devil: John 8:31-47 and the Passover Theme of the Gospel of John." *Trinity Journal* (forthcoming).

Hughes, Philip E. *A Commentary on the Epistle to the Hebrews*. Grand Rapids: Eerdmans, 1977.

Jeremias, Joachim. *The Eucharistic Words of Jesus*. Translated by Norman Perrin. London: SCM Press, 1966.

Justin Martyr. *The Ante-Nicene Fathers*, vol. 1. Edited by A. Roberts and J. Donaldson. Grand Rapids: Eerdmans, 1967.

Keener, Craig S. *The Gospel of John: A Commentary*. Peabody, MA: Hendrickson, 2003.

Keil, Carl F. *The Pentateuch*. Translated by James Martin. Biblical Commentary on the Old Testament, vol. 1. Peabody, MA: Hendrickson, 2006.

Kiuchi, Nobuyoshi. *The Purification Offering in the Priestly Literature: Its Meaning and Function*. Journal for the Study of the Old Testament Supplement Series, vol. 56. Sheffield: JSOT Press, 1987.

Koester, Craig R. *Hebrews: A New Translation with Introduction and Commentary*. Anchor Bible, vol. 36. New York: Doubleday, 2001.

Kraus, Han-Joachim. *Psalms 60-150*. Translated by Hilton C. Oswald. Minneapolis: Fortress, 1993.

Ladd, George Eldon. *A Theology of the New Testament.* Rev. ed. Grand Rapids: Eerdmans, 1993.

Lünemann, Göttlieb. *Critical and Exegetical Handbook to the Epistle to the Hebrews.* Translated by Maurice Evans. Meyer's Critical and Exegetical Handbook to the New Testament, vol. 9. New York: Funk and Wagnalls, 1885.

Marshall, I. Howard. *Last Supper and Lord's Supper.* Exeter: Paternoster, 1980.

_____. *The Work of Christ.* Carlisle: Paternoster, 1969.

Melito, Bishop of Sardis. *On Pascha and Fragments.* Edited by Stuart George Hall. Oxford: Clarendon Press, 1979.

Moffatt, James. *A Critical and Exegetical Commentary on the Epistle to the Hebrews.* International Critical Commentary. Edinburgh: T&T Clark, 1924.

Moo, Douglas J. "The Problem of Sensus Plenior." Pages 175-212 in *Hermeneutics, Authority, and Canon.* Edited by D. A. Carson and John D. Woodbridge. Grand Rapids: Zondervan, 1986.

_____. *The Old Testament in the Gospel Passion Narratives.* Sheffield: Almond, 1983.

Morris, Leon. *New Testament Theology.* Grand Rapids: Zondervan, 1986.

_____. *The Apostolic Preaching of the Cross.* 3rd ed. Grand Rapids: Eerdmans, 1965.

_____. *The Atonement: Its Meaning and Significance.* Downers Grove: InterVarsity, 1983.

_____. *The Cross in the New Testament.* Grand Rapids: Eerdmans, 1965.

Moule, C. F. D. "Fulfillment-Words in the New Testament: Use and Abuse." *New Testament Studies* 14 (1968): 293-320.

Paulien, Jon. "Elusive Allusions: The Problematic Use of the Old Testament in Revelation." *Biblical Research* 33 (1988): 37-53.

Ridderbos, Herman N. *The Gospel according to John: A Theological Commentary.* Translated by John Vriend. Grand Rapids: Eerdmans, 1997.

Spicq, Ceslas. *L' Épitre aux Hébreux.* Sources Bibliques. Paris: J. Gabalda, 1977.

Stek, John. "Biblical Typology Yesterday and Today." *Calvin Theological Journal* 5 (1970): 133-162.

Stott, John R. W. *The Cross of Christ.* Downers Grove: InterVarsity, 1986.

Torrance, T. F. *Divine Meaning: Studies in Patristic Hermeneutics.* Edinburgh: T&T Clark, 1995.

VanGemeren, Willem A. "Psalms." In *Expositor's Bible Commentary*, vol. 5. Grand Rapids: Zondervan, 1991.

Wallace, Daniel. *Greek Grammar beyond the Basics*. Grand Rapids: Zondervan, 1996.

Wenham, Gordon J. *The Book of Leviticus*. New International Commentary on the Old Testament. Grand Rapids: Eerdmans, 1979.

Wiles, Maurice F. *The Spiritual Gospel: The Interpretation of the Fourth Gospel in the Early Church*. Cambridge: Cambridge University Press, 1960.

Young, Frances. "Typology." Pages 29-48 in *Crossing the Boundaries*. Leiden: E. J. Brill, 1994.